Who Killed Leanne Holland?

Who Killed Leanne Holland?

One girl's murder and one man's injustice

Graeme Crowley & Paul Wilson

NEW
HOLLAND

First published in 2007 by New Holland Publishers
Sydney

Level 1, 178 Fox Valley Road, Wahroonga, NSW 2076, Australia

newhollandpublishers.com

A record of this book is held at the National Library of Australia.

ISBN 9781742570228

Publisher: Martin Ford
Production: Linda Bottari
Project Editor: Michael McGrath
Editor: Belinda Castles
Designer: Hayley Norman

10 9 8 7 6 5 4 3 2

Keep up with New Holland Publishers:

 NewHollandPublishers

 @newhollandpublishers

Dedicated to Leanne Holland, Graham Stafford and the Stafford Family: all of whom have suffered a grievous injustice.

Acknowledgements

Many people were instrumental in helping us produce this book.

We would particularly like to thank Robyn Lincoln and Sue Crowley, both of whom provided considerable support and encouragement during the many years of the investigation and the development of this book. This book would not have been possible without their ongoing support. Robyn also provided extensive and invaluable editorial input.

Many journalists assisted us in bringing the case to a wider public, but two in particular deserve special mention. Darrell Giles from Brisbane's *Sunday Mail* and Greg Carey from Radio 4BC provided a great deal of support as well as extensive coverage of the case itself. Their media reports resulted in a number of people coming forward with additional information surrounding the case.

Over a number of years, students in Professor Wilson's Miscarriage of Justice course at Bond University explored the case in great detail and provided valuable insights into some of the forensic and investigatory issues. Some of these students were police officers whose insights were invaluable, but who would prefer to remain anonymous.

Special thanks are due to former Victorian detective Gordon Davie and ex Scotland Yard police Superintendent Robin Napper, whose insights into crucial forensic material associated with the Stafford case helped us immeasurably.

Most of all, we would like to thank all those members of the public who showed us that they were vitally interested in miscarriages of justice by writing or phoning us with encouragement and support. We used to believe that few people in our society were interested in injustice, but we have been proven wrong.

Finally, thank you to the staff of New Holland, in particular Michael McGrath for his persistence and editorial suggestions.

Contents

Preface

Lindy Chamberlain, Kelvin Condren, Alexander McLeod-Lindsay, Edward Splatt and more recently Andrew Mallard, John Button and Frank Button are just some Australians who have suffered gross miscarriages of justice by being convicted of crimes they did not commit. In each of these cases, subsequent investigations have shown that police and forensic experts made major mistakes, resulting in the conviction of an innocent person.

Some forensic experts and police investigators are fond of saying that their techniques are now so sophisticated that it is all, but impossible for similar miscarriages of justice to occur. Forensic science developments and new investigation techniques – advances in DNA profiling, new blood typing, crime scene reconstruction or sophisticated ballistics analysis – are increasingly seen as a panacea to the mistakes of the past and appear to give police an edge in solving violent crime. Despite these advances, forensic mistakes continue and innocent people are convicted by a justice system that stacks the odds against them.

There are at least two reasons for the persistence of major miscarriages of justice in Australia.

The first relates to our adversarial legal system. Inherited from Britain, the system is designed, at least in theory, to seek out the truth. In the modern world, however, lawyers tend to fight each other and point-score. To this end, they use forensic science and forensic 'experts' to gain ascendancy over the other side rather than to pursue truth and justice impartially. Sadly, trial processes, as they play out in front of juries in courts today, have become more a matter of salesmanship than a quest for the truth. It is often the case that the most eloquent lawyer wins.

The second reason revolves around how the police and prosecution mount a case against a suspect. Natural justice is supposed to ensure that a suspect receives a fair trial and that all evidence, for and against the suspect, is presented to the court. It is our view that the adversarial system gives police enormous discretion over what evidence is followed up or ignored and over which suspect is eventually interrogated, detained and charged.

Unlike the system of justice in most European nations, where a judge or non-police official independently oversees the process, Australia's adversarial procedures allow the police to cull the evidence they collect. Unless the defence is able to pour substantial resources into their own investigation, the jury will have no idea that what is presented to them by police and prosecution is potentially distorted. In the worst-case scenario, evidence may have been illegally obtained or fabricated. However, the evidence does not have to fall into this category to give a misleading impression to a jury.

The Stafford case exemplifies both of these flaws in police and legal procedures, and this is one of the main reasons why this book was written. We believe that the conviction of Graham Stuart Stafford for the murder of Leanne Sarah Holland is a significant miscarriage of justice in the Australian judicial system. It is an even greater and unnecessary travesty of justice when it is obvious that the criminal justice system and forensic science appear to have learned very little from the mistakes made in the Chamberlain, and other cases, involving convictions of innocent people based almost entirely on forensic evidence.

Paul Wilson, a criminologist, has written a great deal on wrongful convictions in murder cases. He became involved in this case because he believes that, more than any other case in recent years, it shows how easily such travesties can come about – and how difficult it is to correct such mistakes. Graeme Crowley, a former police officer who served in the Queensland force for twelve years – spent many years investigating the facts surrounding the murder of Leanne Holland and the police case against Graham Stafford. He, too, is convinced that the criminal justice system has failed utterly in this case. So they are both drawn to the inescapable conclusion that not only has the life of an innocent man been destroyed, but a violent sexual killer has escaped justice.

The brief facts are that Leanne Sarah Holland, twelve years of age, went missing on Monday 23 September 1991 from her home at 70a Alice Street in Goodna, an outer western suburb of Brisbane. Her body was found three days later, ten kilometres away, dumped on a bush track at Redbank Plains. She had been viciously battered to death. It is possible that she was sexually interfered with and tortured. She had been apparently burned in a number of places, perhaps with a cigarette, and marks may have been carved into her skin after she died. It was a horrendous crime and all the more brutal given the child's age.

Graham Stuart Stafford, the de facto partner of Leanne's older sister Melissa, was arrested for the murder five days later on Saturday 28 September 1991. Stafford has spent the intervening years as a prisoner in Queensland gaols, serving a life sentence for a crime he maintains he neither committed nor was connected with .

The police allege that Stafford murdered Leanne sometime between 8 a.m. and 4.45 p.m. on Monday 23 September in the house at Alice Street. He supposedly secreted the body in the boot of his car before dumping it at Redbank Plains early on the morning of Wednesday 25 September. Although there were no eyewitnesses, no confession and no motive, he had opportunity and there was forensic and circumstantial evidence connecting him to the crime. Tyre marks, alleged sightings of his car at the crime scene, lies told to police, a maggot said to be found in the boot of his car and a missing hammer all formed part of the Crown's case. The defence case was straightforward. Stafford was not involved in the disappearance or the death of Leanne. Graham claimed Leanne left the house where they lived together early on the Monday morning and was never seen again.

Graeme Crowley first became involved in the case in late 1992 when he was a licensed private inquiry agent operating in the Brisbane area. Stafford's parents, Eric and Jean, came to him by way of a referral from a firm of solicitors for whom Crowley had previously worked. They told Crowley that they knew within their hearts that their son was innocent because he had continually assured them he had nothing to do with the crime and they believed him – unshakably. Stafford's mother Jean said that when Graham was arrested they did not know all the details of the allegations against him. On the day of his arrest, they telephoned a solicitor who was a friend of a friend. The lawyer strongly suggested that Graham be told to tell the truth and, if he did this, 'he has nothing to worry about'. That was the advice Graham's parents passed onto him, but given the outcome of the trial, they regret very much giving him such naïve advice.

A little later the Stafford family also decided to approach criminologist Dr Paul Wilson. Wilson had a high public profile and was known to speak out on issues relating to miscarriages of justice. He had been vocal in the media about the wrongful conviction of Lindy Chamberlain and that of Kelvin Condren, an Aboriginal man in Queensland who was found to be innocent of a murder for which he spent seven years in prison. Wilson was also known to be critical of the Queensland police generally and in particular of the methods they used to solve some crimes. He spent many hours analysing the transcripts of the trial and spoke to the Stafford family in some detail.

His partner Robyn Lincoln, herself a criminologist, assisted him in these tasks and they came to the same conclusion: the death of Leanne and the media publicity it generated provoked a hasty police investigation with a view to obtaining a quick arrest. As a result, investigation procedures were narrow, leading to the collection and use of weak forensic and circumstantial evidence that wrongly convicted Graham Stafford.

At that stage Wilson and Crowley had not met, though Wilson was aware of some newspaper articles that linked the private detective to the Stafford family's search for justice. Crowley spent some time going through hundreds of pages of trial transcripts and making other preliminary inquiries. At this early stage in his involvement he found the evidence implicating Stafford to be overwhelmingly persuasive. He wanted to go straight to the prison and tell Stafford to confess to his parents and put the family out of their collective misery. Crowley believed Jean and Eric to be wonderful people, deserving of the truth, whatever it might be. They may not have liked what Crowley was about to tell them, he thought, but at least they would be able to get on with their lives.

As Crowley delved deeper into the material, however, he became intrigued by the irregularities and inconsistencies in the police case, which comprised evidence that was almost entirely circumstantial or of a questionable forensic nature. He believed in a 'fair go' and, to his mind, Graham Stafford had not received this. There had been little or no cross-examination of the witnesses; the forensic evidence lacked credibility; and, at least in Crowley's eyes, the personality profile of the killer simply did not fit Stafford's character or history.

Some months later, Graeme Crowley the investigator met Graham Stafford the convicted murderer. The young man continued to deny any involvement in Leanne's death. He did not speculate on what Leanne may have done that day or what the police said happened. He simply told Crowley that he did not kill Leanne and had no idea who had. He repeated his claim that Leanne walked out of the house early on the Monday morning to go to the local shops and he never saw her again.

Crowley's tenacity lost him friends in the police service. He was perceived by some as being a 'bleeding heart' and heard rumours whispered about him and his relationship with the Stafford family. One such blatant lie was that the family home had been transferred into Crowley's name to pay his fees. The truth was that by the time the small amount of money that Eric and Jean Stafford had provided for investigations was spent, the detective was sure that he had found serious and significant discrepancies in many areas of the police investigation. He had never taken on unpaid work before and the likelihood of getting further monies in this investigation looked remote. Yet, he was unsettled by the case and decided to pursue it at his own expense.

Early in 1993, Crowley approached detectives in Brisbane's western suburbs who were involved in another murder investigation at that time. He wanted to explore any possible connection between that murder and the killing of Leanne. He expressed concern that there may have been a miscarriage of justice in the earlier case and explained his suspicions of a potential link between the two murders. As a result Crowley became the subject of a complaint to the detectives' superiors that he was interfering in an ongoing police investigation. The complaint came to nothing, but Crowley was suspicious and angered by the overreaction of the police. Paradoxically, police indifference to his inquiries had the same effect – he became even more determined to press on with his investigation of Leanne's murder.

This book tells the story, uncovered by two men convinced a miscarriage of justice had occurred, of a police investigation conducted hurriedly and no doubt under extreme pressure to produce a result. It is a story of evidence being selectively introduced, which implicated Stafford as the killer. It is also the story of evidence which existed at the time of his trial showing that Stafford did not and could not have killed his girlfriend's young sister.

Beyond that this story reveals other innocent victims of our criminal justice system. Leanne Sarah Holland is one such victim. Her family members and friends have to deal, every day, with the loss of their young loved one.

The Stafford family has also lost a loved one; for while Graham is alive, he is serving a life sentence and has been stigmatised as a vicious killer. His family has to endure the pain and shame of their son's incarceration. It is fair to say that truth and justice are also victims in this case. Most significantly, the real killer is still enjoying his freedom, courtesy of errors in our legal system that condemned an innocent man, Graham Stafford, for the crime that somebody else actually committed.

1

The family

Leanne Sarah was the youngest of three children of the marriage between Terry and Sandra Holland. She was born on 1 October 1978, and died in the spring of 1991, just a week short of her thirteenth birthday. Leanne's parents separated when she was a year old. They had been living in northern New South Wales when Terry took the children and returned to Goodna. Sandra remained in New South Wales and Leanne last saw her mother when she was aged four. Terry became her sole parent and guardian, the only one Leanne was to know as she grew to adolescence. Leanne's brother and sister were both older; in 1991, her brother Craig was 23 and her sister Melissa was 20. Craig worked as a labourer for a removalist business and Melissa as a computer operator at a manufacturing business.

To her family and friends Leanne was a happy-go-lucky girl who enjoyed life. She had many friends and no apparent enemies. Although only twelve, Leanne had already had boyfriends, including some a few years older. The police inquiries, however, failed to show that she had any known steady boyfriend at the time of her murder. Despite this there were rumours about a seventeen- or eighteen-year-old male ringing her constantly shortly before her death, although her father denied these claims when he gave evidence at the trial. Melissa, however, said she was aware of a male telephoning the house up to three times a week to speak with Leanne, but she did not know his name.

At the time of her death, Leanne was in grade eight, her first year of secondary school, at Redbank Plains High School. She was a popular member of class, but her teachers described her as 'an average student'.

During her last months, Leanne participated in the Rock Eisteddfod national school program, aimed at educating children on the dangers of drugs through a musical stage show. It was considered a prestigious event in the school calendar and, as Leanne enjoyed music, she was a natural choice for the choir.

In many respects, Leanne was no different to other children of her age. She was going through an exciting, changing and perhaps rebellious period in her life – discovering boys, music and freedom, the walls of her bedroom covered in posters of the latest bands.

It is not clear whether Leanne was sexually active or not, as she had never approached her sister Melissa about contraception or sex-related matters. Yet, letters written to Leanne by her friend Trisha Lynch and later found by Melissa discussed sexual activity. She did appear to have minimal parental supervision, was allowed to come and go as she pleased, and was being contacted by boys much older than herself.

Following recent publicity surrounding the case, one of Leanne's former schoolteachers wrote a letter to the editor of *The Weekend Australian Magazine* in response to an article (14–15 January 2006). The following is an edited extract from her letter:

> The periodic reporting of Leanne's case, relating mostly to the appeals of her convicted murderer, always opens an incredible sadness in me. I was one of Leanne's English and Home Class Teachers at Redbank Plains High School in 1991. I saw her every school day, in the morning for roll class and/or for our English lessons …
>
> I was staying at my mother's on the Gold Coast, when Leanne's face flashed up on the TV news as a missing teenager. My first thought was, 'That would be just like her, to run away.'

Watching the report in some shock, in any case, I watched police carrying garbage bags of things out of her home. I thought that is not something police do for a missing person; that is, gathering evidence like that.

I cannot give you a proper time frame, but I recall this precisely. In the weeks before Leanne was murdered, her behaviour changed significantly. She was suddenly surly, uncooperative and lazy in class. While I had been teaching for only four years, my first reaction to her behaviour was that she had experienced some 'sexual awakening'. I had seen it with teenagers in my classes before. It was a complete personality change. Physically she changed as well, in the sense that her child-self was replaced with a more 'knowing persona'. I felt she, to some extent, enjoyed the attention of being labelled a 'trouble maker'.

Frequently she would enter the classroom with no books, pens or anything. A few times I asked to check her school bag and her books were there. I was bewildered why she would lie to me about something so insignificant. On one occasion, she returned to class with her friend's bag and pretended that it was hers. The strange thing was that (I recall clearly one of them, but it seemed like several other girls were a part of this) her friends seemed desperate to conceal 'her conspiracy'. Leanne's reason for not having her school supplies was always, 'I stayed at my auntie's place last night' …

I tried talking to her, telling her that I wanted to help her. Leanne took to just smiling at me, like she knew a secret. I appealed also to her friends to talk to me as well. Could they tell me what was happening in her life? They too would tell me to 'not worry, she just likes to stay at her aunt's place'.

I explained the dramatic change in Leanne's behaviour to the Deputy Principal. She in turn consulted the Head of Year. I had the belief that Leanne's father was contacted, because I had the impression that the existence of the auntie and Leanne staying with her, was confirmed. Leanne would certainly have been counselled and consulted about her behaviour. My superior reported back to me, that I was not to worry about things. Leanne just liked to stay at her aunt's place. I was asked if I was aware of Leanne's family past, i.e.: I believe her mother died tragically. I said I did, and this was implied to be part of 'the problem', and that Leanne was seeking female companionship in her auntie and still recovering from the loss of her mother.

Leanne's behaviour was frustrating. I felt a bit angry at her, I also felt like I was failing her, in that she did not feel I was the sort of person she could talk to (wasn't that what Home Class teachers were for?) When I saw she had disappeared, my first reaction was that she had escalated her somewhat attention-seeking behaviour, to the point of running away from home. (The sight, however, of the police and garbage bags, made me realise she was probably in more serious trouble.)

After Leanne's funeral and the arrest of Graham Stafford, the story at the school was as follows: Leanne's sister's boyfriend (Stafford) had been putting the hard word on Leanne to have sex with him. He was harassing and pursuing her. Her reaction was to go and stay at her aunt's house to get away from him. Her friends at school knew the situation and urged Leanne to confront and 'threaten' him that if he did not stop, she would go to the police. Her friends knew that the Monday Leanne disappeared was the day she decided to confront Stafford, because he had a rostered day off …

I can recall Leanne's friends throwing themselves on her coffin as it left the church at her funeral. After hearing 'the story', I had always presumed they were not only devastated by her murder, but also by guilt that they had kept her secret, and, if the story was true, encouraged her to confront this dangerous man on her own … It has simply always been on my mind that Leanne's disappearance was not a sudden, random incident. My observations of her changed behaviour leading up to her murder, I believe, must give some credence to the fact that something was going on in her life to cause such dramatic changes.

If Graham Stafford is not the actual killer, I still wonder if his alleged harassment of Leanne forced her into the situation where she 'randomly' met her murderer. That is, did she really run away from home or go to the shops that day to get away from him?

As indicated by her teacher, being the child of a working parent meant that much of the time Leanne was left to fend for herself and was responsible for her own meals and laundry. She seemed to care little for tidiness and her bedroom was generally a disorganised mess. To save washing sheets, Leanne slept beneath a doona and sometimes fell asleep in front of the television in the lounge room, or downstairs in her father's bedroom. There was no discernible pattern; she simply slept where it took her fancy. Some of her clothes were in her bedroom and some were stored in Terry's room underneath the house. She also watched television whenever she felt like it.

It was not unusual for Leanne to spend several nights at a time away from her home. She frequently stayed with friends. Terry claimed he insisted that she always tell him where she was staying. Indeed the family made no inquiries about Leanne's whereabouts on the night of the last day she was seen alive – Monday 23 September 1991. During questioning at the trial, her father admitted he did not know where she had spent the night, but said he had been told she was probably at her friend's place and just accepted this fact.

Terry Holland was aged 46 when his daughter was murdered. He had grown up in and around Goodna; the suburb was his home. He was one of seven children, and his five sisters and one brother still live in the surrounding suburbs. Terry and his family moved frequently from one rental to another, although never very far from the centre of Goodna. When Leanne disappeared, the family had been living at 70a Alice Street for about five months.

Terry was employed as a blue collar worker all his life. For a number of years he held a job in the neighbouring suburb of Wacol at a company that manufactured lead-acid batteries. His usual routine was to finish work at around 4.30 p.m. and spend the rest of the evening at his local hotel, though it was noted he changed hotels frequently. Terry was also a regular darts player. His team would travel around the hotels in the local area, usually one night a week for competitions. Leanne was well known to many of the patrons and staff of hotels in the Goodna area because she often turned up at night looking for her father.

Throughout the investigation into Leanne's murder and during Stafford's trial, Terry maintained that, despite his established pattern of evening drinking, his relationship with Leanne was very close. They spoke regularly by phone and he had raised her and her siblings as a single parent for some years. He claimed they were always able to sit down and discuss any problems that arose between them and said he was not aware of any difficulties between Leanne, Craig, Melissa or Graham.

Given subsequent events, it was significant that Terry told both the police and the court that he had no knowledge of Graham acting inappropriately towards Leanne or anyone else. He also stated that his daughter had not complained to him nor, to his knowledge, to any other person about Graham.

It was established that Leanne had cut her foot in the kitchen of her house some weeks before her death, apparently on a piece of broken glass. Just how badly she cut herself was not determined, but has since been the subject of much conjecture.

Although later considered significant, there was no mention of it in the autopsy report. Leanne is known to have walked through the hallway to the bathroom to clean and treat the wound. She walked through the lounge room, out onto the front patio and downstairs, where she showed the cut to her father. Leanne received no medical treatment for the cut, although it is unclear whether this was simply because the injury was not deemed serious enough. Terry said when he saw the wound Leanne had wrapped it in a piece of cloth. He described the cut as 'a slice about an inch long'. Questioned later at Stafford's trial about the amount of blood, Terry replied: 'I wouldn't say there was a lot. She told me there had been, but when I saw it, not a lot.'

Leanne was not the only person to bleed in that house. Her brother Craig was injured in a pub brawl when he smashed his hand through the glass of a window. The following day he received six stitches to the wound. In his statement to police and in evidence at the murder trial, Craig said he had been drinking at a hotel for several hours when he became involved in a fight.

Sometime after he received the injury, he went home and bathed the wound in the upstairs bathroom. Craig claimed he recalled dropping some blood on the bathroom and hallway floors, but could not remember spilling blood anywhere else. Craig said he had wrapped his hand in his shirt and later disposed of the shirt because it was ruined. After washing the wound in cold water he wrapped it in a tea towel and went to bed. On another occasion, Craig told police that he cut his arm when he smashed a window to get into the house when no one was at home.

Craig Holland had been living in the family home off and on for some time, but in late 1991 had moved into another rental house with mates, leaving Terry and Leanne to share the house in Alice Street. On his single wage, Terry found the rent a burden. Melissa had been living with her boyfriend Graham Stafford for over nine months in the nearby suburb of Collingwood Park.

They obviously enjoyed each other's company, were happy together and between them had bought several household items.

Melissa was concerned about Leanne's lack of discipline and it was mutually decided between Graham, Melissa and her father that they share the house in Alice Street so that Melissa and Graham could help to supervise Leanne.

Graham later told his parents that he was not in favour of going to live at Alice Street, but Melissa persuaded him to go. Around July, the couple moved their belongings in, taking over the main bedroom upstairs from Terry and leaving Leanne in her own room. Terry decided to turn part of the downstairs garage area into a type of granny flat. The three adults agreed that Terry would be responsible for this area while the others would take care of the upstairs cleaning. It was also agreed that Terry could use the shower and toilet upstairs as he wished. As his job involved making lead-acid batteries, he was required to shower at his work before going home each day and only needed to use the home shower on weekends. By the time Graham and Melissa moved in, Terry had moved his television, personal effects and some basic cooking facilities downstairs.

Leanne's sleeping habits and general untidiness were immediately obvious to Graham and Melissa, but Leanne was resentful when they tried to bring some order into her life. If Graham had one complaint about Leanne, it was her untidiness; she gave tidiness a low priority and generally failed to notice that she had even caused any mess. With Graham and Melissa, Leanne was responsible for the upstairs housekeeping, but in the end, at least according to Graham, it was usually he or Melissa who did most of the housework. As Graham liked cleanliness and organisation by nature, he never hesitated to do his share.

As a working couple, he and Melissa had agreed to divide the household tasks. Graham took responsibility for washing the dishes and general tidying up. Melissa cleaned the bathroom and toilet and mopped the floors. Neither of them realised that the subject of domestic cleaning would become such a major focus of a police investigation within a few months of them moving in. Leanne had many friends, but spent most time with Trisha Lynch. Although Trisha was two years Leanne's senior, they seemed to have much in common and Leanne often slept at her place. Trisha had also stayed at Leanne's house for up to a week at a time. Trisha, her mother Elizabeth Collins, her sister and her mother's partner lived in a rented caravan at Goodna, about a kilometre from Leanne's home.

The caravan park stands next to the four-lane Ipswich Motorway and on the banks of Woogaroo Creek. At best in those days, the park could be described as working men's temporary accommodation; at worst, a haven for dropouts, drug addicts and misfits. A visitor to the park is immediately aware of the ever-present noise from the motorway, the closeness of the neighbouring caravans and the run-down, depressing nature of the surroundings.

The park's transient population at this time included Trisha and her family, who came from Tasmania. They had been living at the caravan park for about three months when Leanne was murdered, and returned to Tasmania shortly after. Leanne appears to have had a friendly relationship with Elizabeth Collins, allegedly telling her that Melissa and Graham bossed her around. However, Elizabeth told police that Leanne never suggested that Graham's comments or behaviour were in any way inappropriate.

Some of Leanne's other friends also lived at this caravan park. One was Sean McPhedran, who lived in a small tent in the isolated camping area of the caravan park, on the banks of the creek.

McPhedran's mother and stepfather lived only a matter of streets away, but had asked him to move out several weeks earlier because of his violent behaviour. Although eighteen years old, he became friendly with Trisha and through her was introduced to Leanne.

McPhedran had attended a special school and tended to socialise with younger children because, according to his family, he was more readily accepted by them. He was a big boy for his age and although very overweight, was physically much stronger than the children he mixed with because of their younger years. He was casually employed as a trolley collector at the Redbank Plaza Shopping Centre, situated about five kilometres further west along the Ipswich Motorway. McPhedran did not own a car, but had at least one friend who did and he relied on that friend or on public transport to get around.

A council footpath runs past the front of the caravan park and alongside the Ipswich Motorway. It snakes past the section of the park set aside for camping, where McPhedran was living, and connects the park to the commercial area of Goodna, less than a kilometre away. Leanne would have to walk along this footpath going to and from Trisha's caravan. There is also a dirt track nearby that passes under the road bridge at this point on Ipswich Road. It connects one side of Goodna with the other and leads also to the Goodna Railway Station.

The only other means to cross this busy stretch of motorway is by way of an overhead bridge, but that is over a kilometre away. Many local school children and adults use the dirt track shortcut to access the railway station. From the camping grounds inside the caravan park, there is a clear view of Ipswich Road, the pedestrian footpath and the dirt track.

Less than three weeks after Leanne was killed, McPhedran and the caravan park were to feature prominently in the murder of another twelve-year-old child.

2

A gentle person

Graham Stuart Stafford was born in England on 21 May 1963 to working-class parents. His father Eric was a truck driver and his mother Jean an office worker, later an assistant nurse. The family migrated to Australia in 1969 when Graham was just six. Initially they settled in the northern Brisbane suburb of Ferny Hills, but relocated to Goodna and later neighbouring Collingwood Park when they found that many of their English friends were living in the western suburbs of Brisbane. Graham, his younger sister Stacey and his parents make up a close-knit family. However, when Eric and Jean decided to move to the Sunshine Coast, Graham remained in the west where he had grown up. He had a steady job and was close to all his friends, among them Debra Wilson, Bob Neyndorff and Danny Forest. Up to the time of his arrest Graham saw his family often and kept in regular contact with them by telephone.

Before going out with Melissa Holland, Graham dated Debra Wilson, from 1986 to 1989, and they remained good friends after their formal relationship ended. Debra is now married, but has fond recollections of Graham. She says he is a very gentle, pleasant person who she wrote to and visited throughout his time in prison. At the time of their relationship Debra was a single mother with a young son and recalls Graham was like a father to her child. Debra's young sister also used to stay with them during school holidays and after Graham's arrest, Debra swore in an affidavit that he never took an unusual interest in her sister nor made any inappropriate advances or comments to her. She recalls that the police questioned her relentlessly about Graham's character and sexual preferences.

A workmate of Graham's at the business where they were both employed, Bob Neyndorff, had been his friend for about five years, but they had known each other since school. Another friend, Danny Forest, had known Graham for about ten years and they had shared accommodation for about eighteen months. Danny believes in Stafford's innocence and has stated he will always support his friend.

By the year 2000, Stafford had served over eight years of his life sentence in the Queensland correctional system. His conduct in prison had been excellent, with prison officers describing him as a model prisoner. On one of his regular prisoner status reviews, the consulting psychologist wrote:

> The prisoner's conduct and behaviour during the period under review is reported as good. He is quiet and easily managed, causing no problems. The prisoner's attitude towards staff and other prisoners is also reported as good.

In reporting on a cognitive skills program he undertook, another psychologist wrote:

> Prisoner Stafford attended fifteen out of the sixteen sessions of the program. His attitude towards both the facilitators and other group members was always polite, cooperative and appropriate. Although he was a quiet group member he was consistently supportive of other group members. He completed all homework to a high standard and demonstrated consistent motivation to successfully complete the program. Prisoner Stafford did not experience any significant difficulties in the program and given his attendance, verbal participation and the quality of his written responses, he has successfully completed

the Cognitive Skills Program. It should be noted that, during his participation in the program, prisoner Stafford did not link the concepts presented in the program with his offending, as he continues to maintain his innocence regarding the offence of murder.

Further reports of Graham's exemplary behaviour while in custody are evidenced in a Department of Corrective Services letter to him in March 2000. The letter was to advise him that he had been reclassified to 'low security' status:

> The committee noted that during the period under review you have been involved in the Cognitive Skills Core Program, the Tertiary Preparation Program, a Bachelor of Arts degree, a computer course and the Information Technology Certificate 3. The Committee examined reports in relation to your general behaviour during this review and noted that your response in this area is described as good, quiet and you have a good attitude to staff and prisoners. The Committee noted that you are employed as head librarian and work 7 days per week. The Committee noted you have not incurred any breaches of discipline during the period under review nor been involved in any negative incidents.

Another set of independent observations of the kind of person that Graham Stafford appears to be comes from a former corrective services psychologist, who had this to say when he was interviewed about the case.

> From the information available to me, he is not a psychopath or even a generally cunning individual. I certainly do not think he is someone who could have maintained an obsession for or hatred of the victim and not let it show in some way to his partner, friends or family in some way. Having said all that, I think that if he had done such a horrific crime, he has the

mental capacity to have done a much better job of planning the event and hiding the evidence.

From the evidence again it seems there was extreme aggression and rage used on the victim as well as evidence of a deliberate desire to cause pain and suffering over time. This does not sound at all like Graham's personality. Nor do I think he would do it 'out of character' as they say. It appears his presentation of cooperation with the police is genuine. The detectives Richards and Fynes-Clinton could not get their temporal records of events straight, but were critical of Graham for making errors of memory.

While the rest of the family became naturalised citizens of Australia, Graham did not. This was to prove to his detriment. In November 2006 the Australian Department of Immigration served a 'Show Cause' notice on Stafford for why he should not be deported following his release on parole. Although he had been in Australia for over 30 years, technically he was living in the country on a visa. All his family are in Australia. Any relatives left in England are elderly, deceased or too far removed to know him. Following representations from his solicitors that a further appeal against his conviction was pending, the Department of Immigration and Citizenship agreed to stop proceedings until the outcome of that appeal is decided. At the time of printing, the results of that appeal are not known. What is known is that if the appeal is unsuccessful, it is very probable Stafford will be deported as an undesirable alien. His parents have stated they are too old to return to England; thus, if he is deported, he will be going to a foreign country without the support of a mother and father who, as we will see, have offered him enormous backing and encouragement throughout his ordeal.

The recent publicity about the threat of deportation has yielded responses from others involved with this case. Terry Holland's cousin Bev Miller told the Brisbane *Sunday Mail* in November 2006:

I, for one, and many others in our family have always believed in Graham's innocence. We always believed that eventually the guilty person would be brought to justice. Now we are concerned that this young man is to be deported to prevent the real culprit from being brought to justice.

Others have quite different views. Terry Holland's sister also wrote a letter to the editor of *The Sunday Mail* at that time, stating:

Our family believes Graham Stafford murdered her. We came to this conclusion after attending and hearing all the evidence presented at his trial and confirmed at further court cases. Instead of feeling sorry for this convicted murderer, I would like you to think of Leanne, a 12-year-old girl who loved to sing and dance, being beaten to death by someone she knew. Think of the police officer who found her battered body. More importantly, think of her father Terry, who lives with the pain of losing a child in such horrific circumstances. Deporting this convicted murderer would be real justice, and an opportunity for my brother and our families to move forward.

Thus, this murder, like so many others, has left the family and the community bitterly divided.

3

Fear in the neighbourhood

The suburb of Goodna is predominantly a blue-collar neighbourhood consisting largely of honest, working-class families. Today, houses line both sides of the busy four-lane Ipswich Motorway as it follows the original rough bullock track through the adjoining suburbs of Collingwood Park, Redbank and Redbank Plains. Like similar outer suburbs in many cities in Australia, it suffers from substantial social problems associated with industry downturn, unemployment and sheer boredom for many of its younger residents. These problems are exacerbated by the transience of some tenants living in housing commission dwellings, and a lack of the infrastructure and support services that help to create communities from urban wastelands.

Numerous factories in surrounding commercial and industrial suburbs provide jobs for the blue-collar population of Goodna. The suburb also marks the territorial boundary between the local councils of Brisbane and Ipswich. Goodna is hot and dusty because the sea breezes never reach the suburb, making the air generally still and lifeless, with average temperatures hovering around five degrees Celsius above those on the coast. In 1991 a typical Goodna dwelling was a highset weatherboard house on stilts of three bedrooms, one bathroom, a toilet, kitchen, lounge and dining rooms. These highset houses are designed to catch the faintest breeze and are usually set on 24 perch blocks. In addition, lowset and low-cost government housing commission homes are interspersed throughout Goodna. Population density makes many residents familiar with their neighbours' domestic problems.

Leanne's home at 70a Alice Street was similar to the local prototype. Facing almost due north and of a rectangular design, it had weatherboard siding, was highset, and included three bedrooms, an upstairs toilet and shower, kitchen, lounge and dining rooms. The polished timber floors were low maintenance for occupants and landlord. Wooden stairs provided access to both the front and back doors. A patio across the front of the house added to the living area and was almost a necessity in the Queensland climate. Beneath the house, walls partially enclosed the space used mainly for storage and two-car accommodation. The area under the house would generally be considered unsuitable for accommodation without major renovation.

When Terry adapted part of this lower level into his living quarters, his car and those belonging to Graham and Melissa, had to be parked in the unfenced front yard. The shabby appearance of the house, with peeling paint, untidy lawns and a debris-strewn garden suggested to any observer that it was a rental property.

The house is centrally located to Goodna. One disadvantage of the central position of the house was passing traffic, both pedestrian and vehicle, which was constant and noisy, added to by cars and patrons entering and leaving the Cecil Hotel. This popular local hotel was positioned immediately across the road from the house. The hotel has stood on this site for over a century and has been rebuilt at least twice after being gutted by fires. Drinkers sitting in the lounge bar have a clear view of the driveway, yard, patio and front door of the house at number 70a Alice Street. The street runs east-west and approximately parallel to Ipswich Road, although they are roughly 800 metres apart. Queen Street, Goodna's main thoroughfare, runs north-south and intersects Alice Street. Only one house stands between 70a Alice Street and the corner of Queen Street. Next to the hotel and around the corner in Queen Street is a seven-day convenience shop. Staff and patrons of both businesses knew Terry and Leanne Holland.

All these locations, and the fact that the Holland home was in clear view, became important aspects during the course of the investigations into Leanne's murder.

The house was also within easy walking distance of the main business and shopping centre of Goodna: a row of shops in Queen Street, known as St Ives Shopping Centre. This was to the north of the house and only about 500 metres away. Like many other suburbs, the shopping centre contains a number of small businesses including a newsagency, a bakery and a branch of the Commonwealth Bank. All were to play a part in unfolding events. To the south, Queen Street turns into Redbank Plains Road, which snakes its way through the adjoining suburbs of Bellbird Park, Collingwood Park and Redbank Plains. In all, it is about eighteen kilometres long and many people know it as the back road to Ipswich, even though it is only a two-lane bitumen road. Consequently, it carries considerable traffic both day and night. It was just off this road that Leanne's body was found.

On the Brisbane side of Goodna are the suburbs of Gailes and Wacol. For many years, migrants arriving in Queensland were housed in barrack-style accommodation at the Wacol Army Camp, which still faces Ipswich Road. After a settling-in period of six weeks, the migrants were relocated and many of them opted to settle in the immediate surrounding localities, taking unskilled jobs for which English was not a prerequisite to employment.

In comparison with the rest of the Brisbane metropolitan area, the average income for Goodna is at the lower end of the scale, as are average land values and house prices. Neighbouring Wacol is also home to four major Queensland prisons: a remand centre, a women's gaol and a youth detention centre, along with a mental health facility.

Goodna, like many suburbs with a low per capita income and low-cost housing, tends to suffer abnormally high crime rates. In 1983,

Brisbane's major daily newspaper *The Courier-Mail*, summed it up in the headline 'Suburb of Fear'.

Gang warfare in the suburb between blacks and whites had, the newspaper proclaimed, reached alarming proportions. Racial tension was running high and residents feared the outcome. People told journalists they were afraid to walk to nearby shops by day and did not venture out at night at all. Breaking and entering was at an all-time high and there was talk of forming vigilante groups. Nearby Riverview held the dubious distinction of having almost every single house in the suburb broken into during a single year.

Five years later, the crime situation remained much the same with, this time, the 'City of Fear' headline appearing on an article in a local newspaper. During this period, and of direct relevance to Leanne's murder and its subsequent investigation, were two unsolved disappearances that left an indelible mark on the minds of many in the area.

Late in the evening of Thursday 8 May 1986, Sharron Phillips ran out of petrol on the busy Brisbane-Ipswich Highway at Gailes, about two minutes drive from Goodna. Before her boyfriend could arrive to collect her, she disappeared, and has not been seen since. The case might have been forgotten except for the public embarrassment of the police assigned to the case.

Reporters from *The Courier-Mail* were largely responsible for investigations during the initial days and, to the chagrin of police, their findings were published. The police were forced to play 'catch up' each day by following in the steps of the reporters, but every day *The Courier-Mail* would report the results of fresh investigations, staying continually ahead of police investigators. The police finally got their act together about seven days after the disappearance.

Ten years on, in 1996, a *Courier-Mail* reporter Ken Blanch wrote a scathing article on the fiasco surrounding the police investigation:

> It would be a masterly understatement to say that police started off on the wrong foot when Sharron Phillips disappeared. They looked for witnesses in the wrong place for three days. They

searched the wrong spot for physical clues to her disappearance for four. They had her making calls from the wrong public telephone.

They also questioned the wrong soldiers about whether she sought help at Wacol Army Camp … For example, when Sharron's family, led by her Riverview truck driver father Bob, went on a subsequent late shopping night to the spot where she disappeared and stopped passing motorists to ask whether they had seen her on the fateful night, police threatened to charge them with obstructing traffic.

Then there was the matter of where Sharron's car was standing on the side of the road. Police told Bob Phillips to remove it. After it had gone, they marked the spot with a makeshift flag consisting of a chip packet on a stick, but they placed it in the wrong spot. When they eventually searched the right spot a week later, they found Sharron's shoes and rifled wallet in a road drain.

Any chance of obtaining crucial evidence from the crime scene had, of course, gone by then. Today, on both sides of Ipswich Road, a simple sign bearing the words 'Sharron Phillips' marks the spot where she disappeared. Police would be experiencing the fallout over the botched investigation for years afterwards.

Then, on Thursday 2 August 1990, Julie-Ann Gallon disappeared in broad daylight on Ipswich Road at Riverview. Almost certainly she was abducted and murdered. Julie-Ann's abandoned car, with a flat tyre, was found outside a church on Brisbane Road, an extension of Ipswich Road. Aged 27, she worked in the arachnid section of the Queensland Museum and left behind eighteen horses, three dogs, nine puppies, a cat and a pet rat. At any other time, Julie-Ann's disappearance would have been seized upon by the media, but it was overshadowed by the invasion the previous day of Kuwait by Iraq. It finally made the front page of *The Courier-Mail* five days later, on Tuesday 7 August 1990, under the headline: 'Woman Missing Where Sharron Phillips Vanished'.

While the world held its breath over the Kuwaiti crisis and the threat of local fuel price increases, Brisbane citizens, particularly women, were concerned about travelling alone through the city's western suburbs. The Royal Automobile Club of Queensland took the unprecedented step of instructing their service vehicles to attend all breakdowns involving women travelling alone, regardless of whether the person was a RACQ member or not. The media piled on the pressure for a quick resolution to the cases of the two missing women. Police were well aware they would be under close media scrutiny should any other women disappear, particularly in the western suburbs. These two unsolved cases may help to explain why, when Leanne Holland was reported missing just thirteen months later, the police investigative machine swung immediately into action, determined to produce a quick and decisive result – one guaranteed to satisfy the media, public, politicians and superior officers.

Because of these crimes and the socio-demographic features of the suburb, to an outsider Goodna may seem a tough, even threatening place to live, particularly for a naïve young girl. Leanne, however, had grown up in the suburb, knew it intimately and had no fear of it. It was her home turf where she had a wide circle of friends and acquaintances. Melissa's boyfriend, Graham Stuart Stafford, who was to be tried and convicted for Leanne's murder, felt equally comfortable in Goodna. He could never have imagined that the suburb would be the scene for the tragedy that followed.

4

A normal day

In reconstructing the events leading up to Leanne's disappearance and murder, the preceeding Friday provides a starting point. Friday 20 September 1991 heralded the beginning of the school holidays and Leanne was excited to be going to an end-of-term party at a school friend's house. A sleepover had been organised and Leanne had told her father she would not be home until Sunday night. For some parents, allowing their not yet thirteen-year-old daughter to stay away for two nights would be unacceptable, but it was not unusual for the Holland household.

Leanne dressed in her latest 'going out' outfit – a pair of black MC Hammer pants, white shirt and a black vest decorated at the front with silver diamantés. This was 'the look' for a fashion-conscious teenager in the early 1990s; one that made her appear older than her twelve years. She had borrowed the white shirt from Graham without his knowledge – something she had done several times before.

At the party, Leanne confided to friends that Trisha Lynch, perhaps her closest friend, was thinking of running away because she had been grounded. Leanne said that she was thinking about going with her, but her friends were not able to say later whether she actually intended to leave home or not.

Graham and Melissa also had a big weekend. They headed to the

Gold Coast with friends Bob and Amanda Neyndorff. Amanda later recalled a conversation that took place that weekend when Melissa raised the subject of Leanne wearing Graham's clothes. Graham said he was not concerned about it, but Amanda said it appeared to bother Melissa for some reason. It was casual talk that seemed irrelevant at the time, but later became very significant.

The two couples returned to Brisbane on Sunday afternoon, arriving at Bob's Pinjarra Hills home in time to watch the rugby league grand final. Shortly after the game finished, Graham and Melissa returned home to Alice Street.

On that Sunday night, Leanne slept in a chair in front of the television in the lounge room. Leanne was still there when Graham arose the next morning. Terry Holland drove to work at his usual time of 7.30 a.m. and Melissa left for work about fifteen minutes later. It was a rostered day off for Graham and he stayed at home. Melissa said Graham walked her to her car in the front yard around 7.45 a.m. They kissed and cuddled before she drove away. At that time he was wearing a pair of football shorts but, as the weather was warm, he wore no shirt or shoes. Melissa later told police that when she arrived home from work that afternoon Graham was wearing the same shorts.

School was out for Leanne, but she was definitely at home that morning as Terry, Melissa and Graham confirmed. A number of independent witnesses also saw her at or around her house that day, although the precise times of the sightings are not easy to establish.

One of her school friends spoke with her at about 8 a.m. when he walked passed the house. He told police she seemed her usual happy self and there did not appear to be anything troubling her. Leanne told him Graham was inside the house.

An employee of the Cecil Hotel arrived at work around 8.30 a.m., glanced across the road towards 70a Alice Street and noticed Leanne on the front veranda. No doubt in response to a police question, he said she did not appear to be stressed about anything and later recalled she was playing with a dog. The employee was certain it was Leanne because he had known her and Terry for a number of years. A long-time friend of the Holland family told police that he saw Leanne walking along Queen Street towards the shopping centre at around 9 a.m.

Terry said he took a telephone call from Leanne at about that time. She called from home to ask whether she would be allowed to dye her hair. It was usual for Leanne to call him regularly at work, he claimed. His recollection of the conversation was that he asked her where she was going to get the dye or money and she told him that Graham was going to help her. Terry agreed that she could dye her hair. Later, he told police he detected no anxiety in her voice during their conversation. This apparently innocuous telephone call was to have important ramifications in the investigation into Leanne's death as well as the arrest and conviction of Graham Stafford.

Leanne's best friend, Trisha Lynch, told police that she telephoned the Holland house shortly after 9 a.m. and spoke with Graham, who told her Leanne had walked down to the Goodna shopping centre. The conversation was seemingly innocent and insignificant, but the exact wording was to become crucial later. Trisha Lynch claimed that, after being told Leanne had walked down to the shops, she left a message with Graham for Leanne to come to the caravan park when she returned home. Graham, however, claimed that Trisha said she would go down to the shops to meet Leanne. This was what he later told Melissa then Terry. At his trial, the prosecution claimed that Graham had misled everyone by twisting this simple statement around, in order to distance himself from the crime.

Leanne's former boyfriend claimed that he saw her at the Queen Street shopping centre at about 9.30 a.m. that Monday morning. Another school friend made a later sighting of Leanne, walking along Queen Street from the direction of the shopping centre towards Alice Street. The friend placed the time at around 10.15 a.m.

A number of other people claimed to have seen Leanne both during the daylight hours of Monday and as late as 8.30 p.m. that night. Police were unable to confirm these sightings. While the majority of the sightings have not been recorded here, several stand out.

Confirmation of any one of these claimed sightings would show

Leanne was alive much later in the day than alleged by the prosecution, at a time when it was physically impossible for Stafford to have murdered her. Perhaps the most significant and contentious sighting was at around 11 a.m. at the Goodna branch of the Commonwealth Bank – an incident we shall return to later. A bottle shop attendant at the Weeroona Hotel told police she worked from 9 a.m. to 3 p.m. that day and thinks that she may well have seen Leanne during her shift, perhaps after lunch. The hotel is on Ipswich Road, on the same side and about 500 metres from the Goodna Caravan Park. The attendant previously worked at the Cecil Hotel and knew Terry and Leanne well, although she had not seen either of them for some time. The woman told police that a blonde girl, another girl around the same age and a mature woman who appeared to be the second girl's mother came into the liquor barn. The attendant said she had wanted to ask, 'Is that you Leanne?' but didn't. She regretted not doing so in hindsight.

A Goodna woman approached detectives – as a result of publicity during the police investigation – and told them she had seen a girl fitting Leanne's description outside the Goodna Special School in Queen Street at around 3.15 p.m. She described the girl as having straight blonde hair to below her shoulders, wearing a purple jumper and a black skirt. The woman said she saw the girl talking to an Aboriginal female. She was certain of the time and stated the purple jumper was of one colour.

It is not known if this woman knew Leanne personally, but the clothing she described was identical to that in which Leanne's body was found. No statement was taken from the woman and her information was never revealed to the defence, but a comment in police records notes that this sighting was deemed inconsistent with inquiries and was therefore excluded, presumably because one clear discrepancy is that Leanne's hair was quite curly.

A long-time friend of the Holland family was certain he saw Leanne walking past the Cecil Hotel at about 3.30 p.m. that Monday. This witness was so sure of his observation that he could not be shaken on it six months later at Graham's trial. He was absolutely confident about the day and date. The man had known Terry as a friend for fifteen years and Leanne since she was a baby.

Despite rigorous questioning by the prosecution at the trial, this witness steadfastly maintained that he saw Leanne outside the Cecil Hotel between 3.30 and 4 p.m. on Monday 23 September.

One of Leanne's former boyfriends told police he saw and spoke with her as she entered the Cecil Hotel at 8.30 p.m. that night. The youth later conceded he might have been mistaken about the date of that meeting. He agreed with police that it might have been the night before.

Just as it was imperative to trace Leanne's movements, it was also crucial for Graham's defence to establish his activities on that day. Melissa remembered Graham telephoning her at work between 10 and 11 a.m. She said he seemed relaxed and his usual self during their telephone conversation. In her police statement, she said the conversation was about whether Leanne could dye her hair blonde. Melissa told Graham not to let Leanne use his blonding kit and said she would buy some hair dye on the way home from work. She suggested Leanne call her to tell her what colour she wanted, but she never received a call from Leanne.

Graham took other phone calls that day. Robert Neyndorff told police that some time before 11 a.m. he telephoned the Alice Street house. Neyndorff said Graham seemed relaxed and his usual self during their conversation. Furthermore, he could detect no change in Graham's demeanour from the previous day, when they had returned from the Gold Coast, to when he saw and spoke with him at work the next day. Terry also telephoned at around 11 a.m. and spoke to Graham, who says that he told Terry that Leanne might be at Trisha's place; while Terry's recollection at the trial was that Graham said that Leanne was at the shops.

A neighbour told police he saw a man working under a red car at the side of the Holland house for about fifteen minutes. He thought the time was between 11 a.m. and midday. The car then drove away for a short time, returned and parked in the same spot in the yard. The neighbour went inside and saw nothing further. A later search by police of the interior of Graham's car revealed a receipt from Big

Rooster at Goodna for the purchase of take away food. The receipt was stamped with the date and time of purchase of 11.45 a.m. on Monday 23 September.

After lunch Graham went to visit his friend Arthur Power in the suburb of Collingwood Park, where he and Melissa and had lived before shifting to Alice Street. Power told police that Graham, still wearing his Broncos shorts, had spent half to three-quarters of an hour at his house, 'talking normally' about the previous day's rugby league grand final. He thought Stafford left around 1.30 p.m. Power's daughter arrived at the house while Graham was there and confirmed his presence. She too said there was nothing unusual about his behaviour. Graham's memory of his visit to Power's home differed only in the length of time he spent there, as he told police it was between one and two hours. On his way home he purchased dog food and had his car washed, receiving time and date-stamped receipts: one for Franklins Supermarket at 2.18 p.m. and the other for the car wash at 2.59 p.m. Indeed, a Redbank Plaza shop assistant positively identified Graham as being at the shopping centre at around two o'clock on that Monday.

Melissa remembered talking to Graham again by phone at around 3.30 p.m. but she was not certain who had called whom. Melissa's recollection was that the conversation was just about how his day was going, how her day was and so on.

Melissa arrived home at her usual time of 4.40 p.m. and asked Graham if he knew where Leanne was. He told her Trisha Lynch had called and that he'd told her Leanne had gone to the shops. Trisha had told him that she would also go to the shops to try to find her. Since this was consistent with Leanne and her friend's normal behaviour, Melissa saw no reason to query his response. Terry arrived home, as usual, just before 5 p.m. When he asked Melissa and Graham where Leanne was, Graham told him she was probably at Trisha's place, because Trisha had rung looking for her. When questioned by police, Terry said this was not unusual since Leanne stayed at Trisha's place on a regular basis, just as Trisha frequently stayed at the Holland house.

Then Melissa and Graham went to Franklins to do their weekly grocery shopping. Melissa chose to put the shopping in the back seat of Graham's Gemini sedan rather than in the boot. Later, she was to say that this was solely her decision. Melissa also confirmed that Graham was his normal self and did not seem agitated or upset when she arrived home from work. They chatted generally and Graham mentioned he had cleaned out his car and disposed of some rubbish.

One of Melissa's pastimes was to play netball and Graham used to go along to her games, sitting on the sideline in a folding chair he kept in the boot of his car. As the netball season had ended and Graham was sick of the chair rattling in the boot, he had removed it while tidying his car that day and had later taken it upstairs. He casually mentioned this to Melissa. Later in the evening, he also mentioned to Melissa that he had injured his arm while working on his car.

5

My daughter is missing

On Tuesday 24 September 1991 Graham left for work at his usual time of 6.15 a.m. He later told police he believed Leanne was not at home that morning. After arriving at work, Graham visited the first aid officer to have the injury to his arm examined. After receiving treatment, he remained at work for the rest of the day before arriving home at around 3.30 p.m. At 4 p.m. he went to the Goodna Medical Centre in Queen Street for a doctor to examine his arm injury.

Terry left for work at around 7.30 a.m. that morning and he too believed Leanne was not in the house. At around 8.15 a.m. Melissa went to work, having no idea whether or not Leanne was at home. During the course of that Tuesday, however, Melissa became concerned about Leanne. She telephoned home several times, but there was no answer. She also called her father to see if he had heard from Leanne. Melissa arrived home at 4.45 p.m. and, as Leanne was still not at home, she and Graham drove to the Goodna Caravan Park to search for her. They spoke with Trisha Lynch and her mother Elizabeth Collins, neither of whom had seen Leanne that day or the previous day.

Graham and Melissa were both disturbed because they knew it was very much out of character for Leanne to be away from home for so long without contacting them. As they returned home they met Terry in the front yard. He had just arrived home from work and he too had neither seen nor heard from Leanne. Terry later told police that by then he had started feeling frightened for Leanne. He telephoned as many of her friends as he could call to mind. When he found none had heard from her, Terry, Melissa and Graham drove to the Goodna Police Station in Graham's car to report her missing.

A uniformed police officer took the report and told them that detectives would be assigned to the case and would visit their house looking for clues the following morning. As far as they could tell, Graham was the last person to see Leanne alive and he described her clothing to the police officer, saying she was wearing a purple jumper and black skirt. He could not recall if she was wearing shoes or not. Terry later stated that Graham described Leanne as barefoot. He said Graham's lack of recall on the question of Leanne's footwear grabbed his attention because he believed Leanne would never leave the house without shoes. Terry said he was sure that even if Leanne were just going to the convenience shop two doors down from their house she would wear shoes. After her body was found barefoot, detectives asked him to check Leanne's shoes at home. He and Melissa did so and found that none were missing.

After reporting the matter to police and returning home, it was Terry who suggested they should clean up the house, as the police would be visiting next morning to begin their inquiries.

Graham and Melissa spent some time cleaning upstairs and both said they heard Terry cleaning the downstairs area well into the night. According to a third party, both Graham and Melissa told her that Terry Holland asked them to move Leanne's mattress and clothes from his room downstairs back upstairs to her room, which they did.

At this time, Graham telephoned his parents at their Sunshine Coast home and told them about Leanne's disappearance and that he, Melissa and Terry Holland were very worried about her. His mother Jean said later that on the phone Graham seemed very upset and told his mother he was afraid for Leanne. He was also disturbed because the police seemed to be treating it as foul play. No one slept well in the Holland house that night. It was nearly 48 hours since anyone had seen Leanne and there was still no word from her. Her lack of contact was deeply disturbing. None of her friends had seen nor heard from her either. Leanne had never been away from home this long without telephoning anyone, especially Terry. On one previous occasion, she had phoned him reverse charges, but he told her never to do that again. This time, everyone was hoping she would.

Her family had no reason to believe she had run away. Foul play was suspected, but everyone was hoping for the best. No one knew why the police were already treating Leanne's disappearance as suspicious, but it did help to reassure the family that at least the matter was being taken seriously by the authorities.

Around 6.15 a.m. the next morning, Graham drove off to work as usual. Later, he said that he was upset and distressed about Leanne's disappearance and decided to drive to Arthur Power's home to tell him about Leanne and how worried he was for her.

To reach Power's house, Graham had to turn left out of Alice Street away from his usual direction of travel to work, into Queen Street and then drive west along Redbank Plains Road for about four kilometres before turning off into the suburb of Collingwood Park.

Graham told police that he knocked on the front door of his friend's house, but did not receive an answer. He knew from sharing a house with Arthur for a number of months that his friend was a habitual early riser; but as he did not receive a response to his knocking, he assumed Arthur had chosen to sleep in on this particular day. So, without seeing his friend, Graham said he drove to work. He claimed he retraced his path along Redbank Plains Road back to Goodna, past the intersection with Alice Street and on to his work at Carole Park. Melissa and Terry decided to stay at home until Leanne was found. After Graham left, Melissa made a cup of tea and took it out to the front patio, her concern for Leanne mounting by the minute. She heard then saw Graham's distinctive red Gemini drive from the direction of Collingwood Park along Queen Street and cross over Alice Street.

The time was around 6.40 a.m. Melissa was mildly surprised since Graham had left home 25 minutes earlier and had told her nothing of his intention of doing anything other than travelling directly to work. She was certain it was his car, both from the sound of the exhaust and by its appearance.

When Graham arrived at work, he found he could not concentrate and decided to go home again, but had to wait until a supervisor arrived. He phoned Melissa at 7.10 a.m. to tell her he would be coming home because he was worried about Leanne. He arrived home at around 7.45 a.m.

When Melissa told Graham that she had seen his car earlier on Queen Street, he told her about his visit to Power's and that after he could not raise him, he went to work. Graham later stated, supported by Melissa and Terry's testimony, that he did not leave the house again that morning. Terry had also taken time off work until the issue of his daughter's disappearance was resolved.

Although he prized his CD collection and his car, Graham generally placed little emphasis on material goods. A man of simple needs and pleasures, Graham loved nothing better than keeping his car spotless and enjoying his huge music collection. He had fitted a sunroof to his 1985 fire engine red Holden Gemini sedan and placed an oversize O'Neill sticker across the top of the windscreen.

He kept the car in immaculate condition, its gleaming alloy wheels and its windscreen sticker making it stand out from other cars of the same make and model. He also chose to custom-fit his tyres. All four tyres, which were thirteen inches in diameter, were manufactured by Bridgestone Australia. The front tyres were 185 millimetres wide and were what is known as an RD229 pattern. The rear tyres were 205 millimetres wide and an SF340 pattern. The front tyres were designed for economy and wear, as opposed to the rear tyres, which were there for performance and looks. It is uncommon, except for some young drivers customising their cars, to fit different size tyres.

During the investigation into Leanne's murder, experts within the tyre industry confirmed that having different tyre patterns and sizes fitted on a vehicle was distinctly uncommon. Graham's choice of tyre sizes and patterns was to become crucial in the investigation into Leanne's death and his subsequent conviction.

It was certainly one of the most compelling pieces of evidence to be presented at the trial. It is also memorable as being the basis of perhaps the biggest blunder and example of misinformation in the progress of this case. However, as will be detailed in subsequent pages, it was by no means the only piece of evidence over which serious concerns continue to be raised.

6

A suspect emerges

By 8 a.m. on Wednesday 25 September 1991, the Goodna police were moving swiftly and decisively. Leanne's disappearance was being treated as a murder investigation and a Major Incident Log and a running sheet were set up. These record and summarise the various individual inquiries during a serious crime investigation.

Many parents of missing children in Australia would envy this immediate reaction by police; some would perhaps be angry and bitter at the lack of swift police action in their own cases. The earlier disappearances of women in the area would have been fresh in the minds of the police – perhaps a motivating factor. From outside the case, it is not possible to know whether they were also acting upon confidential information received.

At that stage, there was no body, nor indeed any evidence of a crime having been committed. Nevertheless, a serious crime investigation began just twelve hours after Leanne was reported missing. Senior detectives were recalled to duty on overtime to investigate. Police records indicate that detectives on duty that day lacked experience, perhaps the motivation for calling back the senior officers.

By mid-morning forensic scientists, photographers and fingerprint officers had descended on Leanne's home. The house was thoroughly searched and many items were seized as potential exhibits. In spite of the manpower assigned to the task, only circumstantial rather than direct evidence was ever seized from the house. Terry, Melissa and Graham were taken to the Goodna Police Station where they stayed all day and well into the night, answering questions and providing written statements about the events leading up to Leanne's disappearance.

During questioning Graham was asked to make a statement of his activities on the Monday, two days earlier. He did not request the presence of a solicitor nor was one offered. Graham signed the statement as being accurate and has never disputed its contents. The police conducted an interview and, common to police procedure at that time, Graham's answers were presented in a typed statement prepared by a police officer. In the process Graham's answers were transformed into terminology familiar to the officer typing the statement. This is apparent from the amount of 'police speak' to be found throughout the document. Nothing sinister should be attached to this, but it is noteworthy that the statement jumped around from one issue to another:

I am a single male person 28 yrs of age and I currently reside in a de facto relationship with Melissa Jane HOLLAND at 70A Alice Street Goodna. I also reside at this address with Terrence HOLLAND and also Leanne HOLLAND. I have resided at this address for approximately 3 months.

I recall Monday the 23rd of September 1991, it was my rostered day off work and I stayed home for the day, at 70A Alice Street Goodna, until approximately 12 midday. At approximately this time I left 70A Alice Street Goodna and I travelled to 16 Dobell Street Collingwood Park where I visited a friend namely Arthur POWER. I stayed there for approximately 1–2 hours and after conversing with Arthur POWER I returned to 70A Alice Street Goodna where I remained and worked on my vehicle.

I recall at approximately 8.00 a.m. on that morning I was

approached by Leanne HOLLAND and she mentioned to me that she wished to dye her hair. As a result of Leanne telling me this I obtained a box of hair dye which was left over from when I had my hair dyed and I told Leanne that she could use this dye to do her hair, and that she could wait until Melissa came home so that she could dye her hair.

As a result of this conversation with Leanne, she then rang her father Terrence HOLLAND at his place of work and I did not hear the conversation which she had with her father. After she had made this call to her father, she again approached me in my bedroom of the house and she informed me that she was going down to the shops. She did not state which shops she was going to and I assumed she was going to the shops in Goodna. I did not actually see Leanne leave the house and I would estimate that she left the house at approximately 9.30 a.m. on the 23.09.91.

At the time when she spoke to me in my bedroom she was wearing the following clothing: a purple knitted woollen jumper and from memory she was wearing a skirt which was of a black colour.

When Leanne told me that she was going to the shops she did not inform me that she was meeting anyone down at the shops or how long she would be at the shops for.

At the time when I was talking with Leanne while I was in my bedroom I was wearing a pair of blue football shorts and I was not wearing a shirt. I was also wearing a pair of underpants, however, I cannot recall what colour they were. I have placed these items of clothing in the dirty clothes basket in the house and they have not been washed. I wore the pair of shorts all day and later when I went and visited my friend at Collingwood Park I wore a blue B & D shirt. Also on that day I was wearing a pair of Reebok running shoes, which I am wearing at the present time.

After Leanne left the house, approximately 20 minutes later a friend of Leanne's rang namely Trisha LYNCH and she inquired where Leanne was and I informed Trisha that Leanne had left to go to the shops at Goodna. As a result of me telling Trisha this she told me that she also intended to go down to the shops at Goodna. After this conversation the telephone call was terminated and then I went downstairs and worked on my vehicle which is a Holden Gemini sedan which is red in colour. The work which I was conducting on my vehicle entailed replacing the front shock absorbers on my vehicle and I only got one of these replaced due to the fact that while I was working on my car I pulled the vehicle off the jack and I hit my elbow under the wheel arch. As a result of this occurring I went to the doctor's surgery and I was attended to by Doctor JOOSOB and as a result of this visit I learnt that I had injured the tendon in my left arm.

This injury to my arm occurred at approximately 2.30 p.m. to 3.00 p.m. and I later attended at the doctor's at approximately 4.00 p.m. After attending at the doctor's I returned to 70A Alice Street Goodna and at approximately 4.40 p.m. Melissa returned home and then I accompanied her to Franklins where we did our grocery shopping.

I recall that when I arrived home from my friend's place at approximately 3.00 p.m. and also when we came home from shopping that Leanne was not at home. Due to her not being at home I assumed that she had met up with Trisha LYNCH, and that she would have been with her as she from time to time stays at Trisha LYNCH'S residence.

To my knowledge she did not come home on Monday night and on Tuesday morning at approximately 6.15am I left for work. I did not see Leanne in the house.

On Tuesday afternoon I finished work at approximately 3.00 p.m. and I returned to 70A Alice Street Goodna and when I arrived home there was no other person at the house. I stayed at the house and Melissa arrived home at approximately 4.40 p.m. As a result of Leanne not being home both myself and Melissa waited at home until Terrence HOLLAND came home and we discussed the whereabouts of Leanne and as a result of this both myself and Melissa drove to the Gailes Caravan Park where we located Trisha LYNCH and she informed us that she had not seen Leanne for the last couple of days. As a result of this we returned to 70A Alice Street Goodna where we further conversed with Melissa's father and as a result of this conversation we all attended at the Goodna Police Station to report Leanne as being missing.

On Monday the 23.09.91 at approximately 9.30 a.m. when I last spoke to Leanne, I cannot recall if she was wearing any jewellery or if she was wearing shoes. She was wearing her hair as she always wears it, by that I mean it was still long blonde coloured hair which is permed. At the time when she left for the shops she was not wearing any makeup.

I have known Leanne HOLLAND for a period of time namely 11 months and I have lived in the same household as her for the past three months. During this period of time that I have known her it is not uncommon for her to stay at her friend's place and to my knowledge she always informs her father of her whereabouts. During the period of time that I have resided in the same abode as Leanne I have been able to converse freely with her and I have not had any altercations with her during this time that I have known her. To my knowledge there have not been any arguments between Melissa and Leanne or between Leanne and her father.

At some point during that first day of investigation, Graham appeared to become the sole suspect in Leanne's disappearance. Graham's name first appeared on the police log as Job Number Three at 9 a.m., a mere hour after the investigation began.

This was not unusual since he was the last person known to have seen Leanne, they lived in the same house and he was present when her disappearance was reported to police. It was a logical place to start an investigation and the police would have been criticised had they not immediately questioned him. Detectives were instructed to interview Graham and obtain a statement from him of his movements and knowledge of Leanne's disappearance. By early afternoon police had impounded his car and seized all his clothing for forensic testing. It was at that stage that detectives officially told Graham he was a suspect in the case. Detectives were then instructed to interview Arthur Power about Graham's visit to him on Monday.

7

Azaria revisited

Police Scientific Branch forensic specialist Bill Crick was sent to the Holland house to examine it and arrived at 10 a.m. on Wednesday. Crick holds a Bachelor of Science degree in physics and had at that time been attached to the police scientific section for six years. His role included collecting and preserving evidence of a scientific nature that might assist in identifying offenders. He had attended many crime scenes and the procedures required to preserve any evidence located were second nature to him.

Crick later stated that during his investigation he had acted in accordance with his experience and training and in keeping with standard operating procedure. He kept detailed notes of his observations, from which he prepared a precise written statement. One of his tasks was to search for evidence of blood. Apart from a visual search for actual blood or bloodstains, Crick used the Sangur test strip. Quite simply, this is a small thin strip of plastic, impregnated with chemicals that react by changing colour to the presence of haemoglobin. Blood does not have to be visible to the naked eye to obtain a positive result to this test. The chemical strip also reacts positively to a number of other substance traces, including iron in the atmosphere.

A neighbourhood such as Goodna, which is home to heavy industry, would be expected to react positively to a Sangur test. Terry Holland's job making lead-acid batteries might also be expected to lead to positive results within his home. The Sangur test is designed merely to assist an investigator in the field. If a positive result is obtained, the investigator is expected to take a swab of the suspect trace for more precise testing under laboratory conditions.

The test gained notoriety for its unreliability in the Chamberlain case in the Northern Territory in the early 1980s. The case attracted worldwide attention as Australia's 'baby-dingo' case from the moment that nine-and-a-half-week-old Azaria was reported missing from her parents' tent at the Ayers Rock camping ground.

Despite no motive, no body, no witnesses and no admission of guilt, Azaria's mother Lindy Chamberlain was charged with murder and her father Michael as an accessory. The charges were supported solely by forensic and circumstantial evidence gathered by police. Eventually the Chamberlains were exonerated, although the community remains divided over the case even today.

One legacy of the notorious case is that doubt was cast over not only the Sangur test, but also over some laboratory techniques. The Sangur test allegedly located the presence of blood in the Chamberlains' car, which was confirmed as foetal blood by laboratory testing. It was not until much later that further laboratory tests identified the traces as sound-deadening material sprayed onto the bodywork of the car.

The relevance of this, both the Chamberlain and Holland cases, is the failure of not only the jury, but also of some supposed expert witnesses to understand fully evidence relating to bloodstains and the tests carried out on them. While the evidence of bloodstains in the Chamberlains' car and on other property belonging to them was hotly and effectively contested, it appeared the jury retained the belief that bloodstains had in fact been found. Even after the blood evidence was totally discredited, many people still claim there was blood in the Chamberlains' car.

It is impossible to know what was in the minds of the jurors in either the Chamberlain or Stafford cases, but it is reasonable to suggest that the jurors clung to the first statement that blood had been found as a means of avoiding becoming enmeshed and confused by scientific evidence beyond their comprehension.

Leanne had left a visible blood trail across the patio and down the front steps of the house when she cut her foot some weeks earlier. The trail was still there on 25 September and was immediately noted by Bill Crick. This blood trail was to figure prominently in the police investigation. Crick reported that he found over twenty separate blood spots on the patio and front stairs. The fact that he counted them would suggest that he found them important. At the committal proceedings he informed the court he applied training he had received in assessing the blood splatters to this evidence.

Whether Leanne's cut foot also led to blood being later found on a blanket and tool bag in the boot of Stafford's car is pure speculation, but the blanket and tool bag would form an integral and significant part of the case against Stafford.

For now, the forensic investigations were in their early stages and Officer Crick's statement reflected his initial findings:

> I tested various areas throughout the house, bathroom, hallway, lounge and front stairs. I located spots and stains in these areas, which when tested with a Sangur test strip, gave a positive reaction. The floors of the hallway, bathroom, lounge and kitchen appeared to have been washed. I then examined a red Gemini sedan 539 OXB. I tested various areas on the vehicle for the presence of blood. I received a positive result from the gear lever, the steering wheel, outside door handles on both front doors, inside the boot lid and various items in the boot.

Crick's handwritten notes of the day included the following comment: 'located maroon football shorts in the wash. Jocks in the wash. None located with bloodstains!! Examined other clothing in washing basket – neg!!' These were the clothes that several witnesses stated Graham had worn during the morning and afternoon on Monday.

It is not clear whether Crick's use of multiple exclamation marks in his comments is borne of frustration or is otherwise significant to the investigation.

His initial positive findings led Crick to take swabs from throughout the house. The u-bends were removed from below sinks and all the tiles were lifted from the floor of the bathroom. Crick told investigators that in his opinion the floors of the house had been recently mopped. He had found a mop and bucket half filled with dirty water on the rear veranda. The water in the bucket tested positive with the Sangur test to traces of blood. This would appear consistent with the scenario that someone had killed Leanne in the house and cleaned up her spilled blood.

Had Leanne been slain in the house, as the prosecution claimed at Graham's trial, quite obviously there would have been a need to clean up her blood, but no cleaning items were found to be missing from the house. This left only two apparent options – that Graham used the mop and bucket from the back landing or he left the house to buy other cleaning equipment that he later disposed of. No 'foreign' cleaning utensils or chemicals were found by police or members of the Holland family. Ultimately, the mop and bucket tested negative to the presence of blood, which ruled out the first option.

The positive reactions to Sangur test strips in the home and in Graham's car were not the only damaging evidence discovered that Wednesday by Crick. He also found a live maggot beneath a tool bag in the boot of the Gemini. Oddly, while Crick's written notes recorded the bulk of his activities and findings on that day, they made no reference to this seemingly crucial and ultimately vital discovery. The video camera operator who filmed the contents of the boot of Stafford's car was not told to take footage of the maggot. Dozens of still photographs taken that day also failed to include the maggot.

When asked at the trial why he did not take possession of the maggot immediately, he told the court that he took nothing from the car that day, but preferred to have the car taken to police headquarters where he could examine it more thoroughly. During the subsequent trial Crick apologised to the court, saying, this was 'a mistake' on his part. Fortune favoured Crick, but frowned upon Graham, for the lone maggot did not disappear into a crack or body panel in the intervening 21 hours.

The investigation continued relentlessly, but as is often the case, not all information brought to the attention of police was taken seriously. A resident of Jindalee – a suburb about five kilometres away – reported that she had heard female screams and pleas, together with male voices chanting, from the nearby river bank during the night. Detectives were advised that the information seemed off-beat and should be treated with caution. The result recorded was that there appeared to be no connection with the Holland case. There seems to be little doubt, however, from the police logs, that the police were satisfied that a crime had been committed and they would find a body.

The job log from Wednesday morning recorded that detectives Richards and Fynes-Clinton were nominated as the arresting officers for the investigation. The teams of investigators faced many tasks. Detectives went to the BP car wash on Redbank Plains Road and questioned staff about Graham's visit there on Monday. They were in possession of the receipt showing Graham had washed his car there at 2.59 p.m. that day. Staff were also questioned about Graham's dress and demeanour.

Records indicate police also took possession of a security videotape. What was on the tape was never disclosed, although it was discovered from job logs that it was entered as an exhibit. A detective was assigned to view the contents of the tape, but the tape was not produced at trial and no mention of its contents was made.

8

A grim discovery

S tafford was reinterviewed on Thursday 26 September from around 9 a.m. This interview was videotaped, but was a rehash of Graham's written statement made the previous day. Once again, Graham neither asked for nor was offered the services of a solicitor. He willingly answered all questions put to him. There was at least one curious aspect to the interview. Graham was questioned about his movements on the Monday – about the blood allegedly found in the house and on the items in his car and about the supposed discrepancies in his statement.

He forgot to tell police of a phone call he received from a fellow worker and that he had gone to Franklins and Big Rooster during his day off – on the Monday. They also queried him regarding the date of the doctors visit to check his arm.

At no time, however, did police mention the maggot in the boot of his car. It would have been a significant find, particularly given the nature of the investigation and the fact that there was no apparent food source in the boot of the vehicle, which the maggot would need to survive. Was the failure to inform him about finding a maggot perhaps an 'ace' police were keeping up their sleeve?

Teams of detectives spent many hours that Thursday tracing and interviewing those who attended the end-of-term party with

Leanne the previous Friday.

Then the news arrived that forced all other activities to take a back seat: Leanne's brutalised corpse had been discovered. Two police had been despatched on trail bikes to search dirt tracks in the vicinity of Leanne's home. Ipswich Traffic Branch Officers Dowdle and Reay scoured bushland around Goodna and the surrounding suburbs of Camira, Redbank Plains, Bellbird Park, New Chum and Collingwood Park. Their trail bike engines ran hot as they covered more than 60 kilometres, searching every accessible track and dirt road. Dowdle later said he did not give up because he had a feeling he would find something. Nothing could have prepared him for the grisly discovery ahead.

Sometime shortly after 1 p.m. on Thursday, the police were on Redbank Plains Road, about ten kilometres west of Goodna and travelling east towards Redbank Plains. Near the intersection of Greenwood Village Road, they had completed a westward sweep along the road and were returning, covering the bushland on the other side of the road. Although this particular stretch of road is only about five kilometres from the residential section of Redbank Plains, the adjacent bushland has only isolated pockets of housing.

Other than an occasional bushwalker, pedestrians are very rare, although horse-riders are not uncommon. There is no footpath or cycling path. Anyone venturing along the road on foot does so at his or her own peril due to the consistently high volume of traffic. The bushland does, however, attract trail bike riders. Cars are also often seen parked on the roadside or in the scrub.

During their search, the motorcycle police noticed that the relative isolation and the general scrub terrain created other problems in the reserve. Stolen vehicles were frequently dumped there, the bush was used as an illegal rubbish tip and the more secluded arbours were renowned lovers' lanes. Dowdle and Reay arrived at two more dirt tracks leading off to the left side of Redbank Plains Road. They decided to split up, Dowdle taking the first track while Reay searched the other.

A short distance along the first track, Dowdle found beehives.

He followed the dirt track and travelled up a steady incline toward a rocky outcrop about 100 metres in from the bitumen road. The track became steep with only a thin layer of soil covering its rocky surface. Grass and light vegetation covered the ground between the gum trees, along with bits and pieces of refrigerators, stoves, car bodies and other trash on either side of the dirt track.

It was among this debris that Dowdle saw the body of a female child, lying on her side next to a tree, discarded as if she were a piece of rubbish. She was naked from the waist down. Her upper clothing had been rucked up leaving the lower half of her body exposed. Her skull had been savagely bashed in; her face was unrecognisable. Even though visual identification was impossible, Dowdle was sure the dead girl was the missing child, Leanne Holland. He quickly noted that dried blood covered her body and clothing, but saw no blood on the surrounding ground. Leanne's beautiful, long, normally blonde hair, now appeared to be a rich red, almost auburn colour. The unseasonably hot September weather had accelerated decomposition. Maggots infested the bloated body and flies swarmed noisily around.

The body was hidden from the view of the busy road about 70 metres below by the surrounding undergrowth and the height of the site above the road. The overhead canopy of trees cast sufficient shadow to further hide the body from any casual observer. The speed of passing traffic and the isolation of the site helped this lonely spot in the bush to keep its secret.

Leanne's battered, bloody shell might not have been discovered for days or even weeks had Dowdle not decided to take that track. The two police officers recognised that macabre luck was on their side, knowing that the longer a body remains undiscovered, the fewer clues are likely to be found at the scene. Given the level of putrefaction, neither officer was qualified to estimate the time of Leanne's death, but it was obvious she had been dead for some time. They noticed her outer clothing consisted of a heavy woollen purple jumper and a multicoloured skirt. There was no sign of panties nor shoes.

Dowdle immediately secured the crime scene and called in his discovery by radio to police headquarters. Detectives, crime scene specialists and forensic scientists were soon on their way, including forensic pathologist Rosemary Ashby and scientific officer Bill Crick.

Dr Ashby is a medical practitioner and specialist pathologist who graduated from London University in 1956. She became a member of the Royal College of Physicians in 1958 and of the Royal College of Pathologists in 1982. By September 1991 she had thirteen years' experience in the field of forensic pathology and was in her third year at the Institute of Forensic Pathology in Brisbane. Dr Ashby arrived at the scene and examined Leanne's body.

She observed a young Caucasian girl in early puberty with a mass of curly auburn hair. Ashby certified life was extinct and made a limited examination at the scene before the body was removed for a formal, comprehensive post-mortem examination.

When Dr Ashby described Leanne's hair as a 'mass of curly auburn hair' who would dare contradict her? Later, when confronted with overwhelming evidence to the contrary from a government chemist, she refused to accept that Leanne's hair had not been dyed. In addition, because of her experience and qualifications, few people would challenge her later claim that the body of a young person would not smell as badly as an adult during decomposition. Indeed, as we will see, it would take a brave police officer to point out to her that all dead bodies smell badly regardless of their age and size.

Bill Crick arrived at the scene around 4 p.m., bringing with him a photographer and a video camera operator. All forensic investigators are aware that establishing the exact time of death is crucial to an investigation. They also know it is possible to calculate the time of death in a decomposing body by determining the growth rate of the maggots found on the body.

Maggots grow through a series of stages and their growth rate is directly related to the surrounding air temperature and available food supply. A forensic entomologist with details about air temperatures in previous days can determine the growth rate of maggots in hours and accordingly, calculate the time of death of the person. This procedure is based on the assumption that blowflies lay their eggs (almost) simultaneously with the death of the person. Indeed, blowflies have been observed laying eggs on patients in intensive care wards in hospitals at or just prior to their death.

Crick took maggots from the head and anal areas of Leanne's body. He sealed the maggots in plastic vials, which he marked for evidentiary purposes. According to the evidence given at trial, these vials were numbered 1 and 2.

He also noted a green garbage bag located on the ground, partially under the body, and recognised it as a type found in almost every Australian household. He also saw a cigarette lighter nearby. Photographs taken at the scene by the police photographer show what appear to be three unsmoked cigarettes close to Leanne's body, but records indicate these were not collected by police.

Crick took particular interest in shoe prints in the immediate area and the impressions of tread patterns of at least three different motor vehicle tyres in the dirt on the track leading to where Leanne was found. The tread pattern on the tyres of the motorbikes ridden by the police officers were compared with the impressions in the dirt and eliminated.

Regrettably, the rocky ground did not lend itself to plaster casts being taken, so Crick would have to rely on photographs of tyre and shoe impressions enlarged to their original size. The light was fading and rain threatened so an urgent call went out for a tarpaulin to cover the tyre impressions.

Crick returned to the Alice Street house where he tested everyone's shoes, including Leanne's, for the presence of blood and found that every single one tested positive to the Sangur strips. Crick took possession of a sample of shoes, but none had similar sole patterns to the shoeprints found at the scene.

9

Sexual predator
at large

To a first-timer, a visit to a morgue is an overpowering experience, both of sight and smell, which tends to remain long after the visitor departs. On first glance, the morgue is very much a clinical environment, with tiled floors and walls, bright overhead lighting and a distinct antiseptic odour, similar to the operating theatres of many hospitals. As in these, morgue personnel also wear long green cotton protective trousers and coats, but there the similarity ends.

The main autopsy room consists of a row of stainless steel benches bolted to the floor. The bigger morgues can have up to twenty of these side by side. The tables are slightly slanted so that gravity will draw the flow of human blood and other body fluids into a bucket strategically positioned beneath the drain hole at the end of the table. Between each table sufficient room is allowed to manoeuvre a cadaver-laden gurney. Suspended from the ceiling above each table is a microphone. This enables the pathologist to dictate his or her findings throughout the autopsy.

Shelves of surgical instruments are augmented by other tools not generally seen in an operating theatre. Band saws, circular saws and hacksaws stand ready to perform their grizzly tasks. Missing are the heart and pulse monitors and other machines associated with the vital signs of life. Morgue pathologists have no need of such equipment. The intense human pressure found in operating theatres is also absent – no decisions are made here on procedures relating to life or death. Naked bodies lie on steel tables. They will be forever cold and still.

Dr Ashby performed the autopsy on Leanne's body and recorded her findings, as she had done numerous times before for other cases. She noted a massive wound to the left side of Leanne's head as well as fractures to the front, left and rear of the skull. Leanne's nose was also broken. Almost no part of Leanne's head had not been bashed. Ashby determined her death was caused by at least ten blows to her head with a heavy, blunt object. An adjustable spanner or wrench was also possible. Bruising to Leanne's neck was consistent with her being pinned down while the blows were inflicted on her before her death. Further bruising to the young girl's hands, fingers and arms attested to the ferocity of the attack on her. Ashby concluded that Leanne had fought to protect herself until she had passed out.

Five *piqueres*, or trace marks, were found on Leanne's torso by Dr Ashby, as well as a similar mark on the inside of her left thigh. The marks were outlined in blood. Ashby deduced these marks were carved into Leanne's skin after her death. There were also at least four burn marks on the body, possibly caused by a cigarette or lighter, and these injuries were inflicted before Leanne died. Given the size of these burn marks, Ashby was in no doubt that the victim had suffered excruciating pain.

A wound next to the anus appeared to be caused by an instrument such as a blunt knife. Dr Ashby added that the wound contained foreign matter like grass or dirt. She suggested two possible explanations for this wound – the first, that Leanne's killer had attempted anal intercourse on her and then carved a larger opening to enable him to complete the act. Alternatively, Dr Ashby suggested, the killer could have a sadistic fetish with the anal-rectal region. Ashby was unable to determine whether sexual intercourse had taken place, but there was no injury to the vagina and no sperm was found.

Whatever the findings of the pathologist, an innocent young girl had been savagely assaulted and murdered. In her report to police, Ashby described the murder as a 'sadomasochistic' killing that by its very definition suggested the killer inflicted Leanne's injuries to gain pleasure from the pain and humiliation of his victim. Her report says: 'In such cases, cuts or fine scratches in patterns may be found upon the skin, known as *piqueres*. In this case, they appear to have been done after death and outlined in blood.'

Piquerism is rare. Crowley conducted many inquiries in Australia in an effort to locate police who had seen similar marks in other murder cases. None were found. Eventually, Crowley and Wilson contacted Robin Napper – a former English Police Superintendent, currently a forensic consultant living in Perth.

Napper's CV was formidable. As well as having 31 years' investigative experience, he had lectured at the UK Police College and FBI facility at Quantico, USA. He had acted as a consultant to the police forces of Singapore, Hong Kong, Oman, Jordan, Romania and Thailand. He was a manager in a task force that reviewed over 200 'cold case' murder investigations in Britain and was brought to Australia to advise police authorities about establishing a national DNA data bank. Napper observed, in his report on this case, that piquerism:

> ... is a sadistic sexual perversion, usually found only in older offenders who have a history of violence and sexual offending. This coupled with the possible cigarette burns, points to an older type of offender who smokes.

Samples of Leanne's blood taken during the post mortem showed a blood-alcohol content of .048 per cent, slightly under the legal limit to drive a motor vehicle. Dr Ashby explained this level of alcohol might be attributable to decomposition of the body. It might also be attributable to Leanne consuming alcohol prior to her murder, but that issue was apparently never raised publicly.

The absence of food in the stomach led Ashby to record that the child had not eaten for at least three hours before death. There was no evidence to show that inquiries were conducted to determine whether Leanne had eaten breakfast on the Monday morning. If she had, then she must have been murdered sometime after 10 a.m. that day, at the earliest.

Dr Ashby concluded that Leanne died on or about Monday 23 September 1991. Whether she arrived at this conclusion independently or because she was told that this was the last time the child was positively seen alive is not clear and was never clarified in court or elsewhere. It is normal procedure for investigating police to brief the medical examiner on when the dead person was last seen alive. Establishing the time of death as accurately as possible is critical.

The police rely heavily on this information to determine who had the opportunity to commit the murder. Certainly, the wording of Ashby's statement: 'the state of the body would be in keeping with death on or about 23 September 1991' is consistent with her being told Leanne was last seen alive on that Monday, but does not rule out that she reached that conclusion independently as a result of her examination.

The clothing from Leanne's body was tagged and sealed in plastic bags for possible production as evidence in court. Specimens of blood and other bodily fluids were also taken along with samples of Leanne's hair. Numerous photographs of her body and its injuries were taken.

At the same time, the vast resources of the Queensland Police Service swung into action to find the person responsible for her savage murder. Teams of detectives were assembled. The media liaison team was briefed. News releases were composed to alert the public to the crime and to launch an appeal for information. There was now intense pressure on investigating detectives to resolve this matter quickly and, in the process, improve the recently tarnished crime-detection reputation of the state's police.

10

The suspect
is cornered

Documented evidence indicates that the detectives investigating Leanne's murder already had a suspect firmly in
their sights – Graham Stuart Stafford.

Forensic scientists had found blood traces on items in his car and in
the house where both victim and suspect lived. Initial tests indicated
blood had been on his shoes – in fact on all the shoes in the house.

Police suspected Graham had helped Leanne to change her hair
colour from blonde to auburn on the day she died. Tyre patterns
found in the dirt near her body were distinctive and emerging witness
reports hinted that a car similar to his was seen near where the body
was found. On top of all this, it seemed to them that Graham had lied
to police about his movements on the last day Leanne was seen alive.

On Friday 27 September, Crick returned to the Holland house and
took further swabs for scientific testing. He also seized plastic garbage
bags from the kitchen.

The garbage service for Alice Street at that time was on Tuesday
mornings. Both Terry and Melissa later told police they did not put
the wheelie bin out to be emptied on the Monday night. By inference
at the trial, the Crown alleged Graham put out the bin and thus was

able to dispose of evidence, but significantly, no blood traces were found in the wheelie bin to support this theory.

In any analysis of the case, it is significant that Crick did not subsequently obtain a positive result to blood tests on any of Graham's clothing or shoes. Yet he had seized all the shoes in the house and, according to the Sangur tests, all of them tested positive to blood – a confusing yet significant discrepancy. After his examination was complete, a police video cameraperson recorded Crick re-enacting his examination of the house and Graham's car. During the re-enactment, Crick referred to the various Sangur tests he performed and the positive results he obtained throughout the house and car.

As previously mentioned though, the Sangur strip is only a presumptive test that must be confirmed by more precise analysis in a laboratory.

The crime investigation had been underway for two days. Detectives had a suspect and the media was sniffing a story. Someone was sufficiently confident of the facts by the Thursday afternoon to leak information to *The Courier-Mail*, which ran the following story on Friday morning under the headline:

GIRL MURDER CLUE CAR, LIGHTER MAY HOLD KEY
Police investigating the murder of 12-year-old Goodna girl Leanne Holland are confident a bloodstained car, a cigarette lighter and footprints will help identify her killer.

The car was discovered on Wednesday and was impounded while police scientific experts carried out tests. Southern Region crime chief Detective Inspector Wayne King said two policemen on trail bikes found the body at 1.40 p.m. yesterday. They had been among a large team of police officers involved in the search for Leanne. Inspector King said the body, which was unrecognisable, was naked from the waist down.

On the same day, in another newspaper, Inspector King had reportedly told journalists that: 'police had not yet attached any significance to a cigarette lighter found near the scene of the crime and ruled out as "totally incorrect" media reports of a connection between the murder and a bloodstained car apparently found in the Goodna area'.

Inspector King also described Leanne's killer as 'certainly not the full quid', the meaning of which was not clarified.

As the investigation continued, police visited the convenience shop around the corner from the Holland home, to ask if Graham had bought any cleaning goods on Monday, with a negative result. As indicated earlier, no evidence was ever uncovered that Graham purchased additional cleaning products. At 12.30 p.m. on that Friday, detectives questioned Melissa again with specific questions about Graham. Their questions related to hair dye, his sexual preferences and the contents of the vanity cabinet in the bathroom.

Other forces were also at work. An anonymous female telephoned police to say that she had heard from 'a friend of a friend' that Leanne went to school that year with bruises to her face. Leanne had supposedly told her friends she had been assaulted by her sister's boyfriend.

Someone, it appeared, had it in for Graham; the allegation was proved false when police interviewed teachers, staff, family and Leanne's friends. It was never discovered who made the call nor what their motive was.

By Saturday 28 September, the investigation was winding down. This was evident by the small number of job logs being generated and the fact that they almost exclusively related to Graham. They included instructions to find out his reaction to the news of Leanne's disappearance then death and what changes had been made to the bathroom of the house.

Then police received the information they had been waiting for. Scientific experts told them that the blood spots in the bathroom of Leanne's house, on a canvas bag and blanket in Graham's car matched blood found on the front steps. This blood was found to be the same type as Leanne's, but was not conclusive evidence, as 48 per cent of the population share the same grouping. It was well into the next week before the scientists were able to show almost conclusively that it was Leanne's blood. A blood expert was also able to tell them that a hammer belonging to Graham had tested positive to blood, but that it could not be determined whether the blood was human.

Police, however, had the evidence they had been seeking. Leanne's blood appeared to have been found on items in the boot of Graham's car. Now all they had to do was show how and where he killed her. Graham was interviewed again, the video camera rolling as he answered all the questions put to him. By this time, the police were treating him seriously enough to give him the standard official warning that he was not obliged to answer any further questions or make any statement, but that anything he said could be recorded and used in evidence against him.

To a solicitor or a layperson with some experience of the law, that warning would indicate that police probably intended to arrest the person at the end of the interview. In such instances, it is rare for a solicitor to advise a client to continue to cooperate with the police.

Once again, Graham did not have a lawyer present. He believed he didn't need one and no-one tried to persuade him otherwise.

The interview is memorable only by what it failed to produce. Graham continued to deny any knowledge of Leanne's death, as these extracts show:

Detective Senior Constable Fynes-Clinton: All right, and do you agree that we spoke to you, in fact we did an interview on tape, the following morning and … you told us that you had no knowledge of how the blood came to be there and that you had no part in the disappearance of Leanne Holland. Is that what you said that time?

Stafford: Yes, it's the truth.

Fynes-Clinton: All right then. All right – are you upset at the moment Graham, are you?

Stafford: Just a little bit – just – it's okay.

Fynes-Clinton: Do you feel you can go on and answer questions at the moment?

Stafford: Yep. I've got nothing to hide.

Fynes-Clinton: All right then. Now … I understand that since we interviewed you last time ... the body of a female was located in bushland off Redbank Plains Road near the intersection of Greenwood Village Road at Redbank Plains. Are you aware of that?

Stafford: Um (nods).

Fynes-Clinton: All right, and are you also aware that the body found was identified as that as the missing person – Leanne Sarah Holland?

Stafford: (sobs) Yes.

Fynes-Clinton: All right. Now the scene up there – the bushland was also examined by police on the Thursday afternoon, and a number of items were located ... at the scene – there was some tyre tracks – at the scene – they have been photographed, and the clothes that were on the body have been taken possession of and there was a green plastic bag under the body at that location. All right. Do you understand what I've said there?

Stafford: Yes.

Fynes-Clinton: All right then ... also at ah ... when we went up to the scene on the Thursday afternoon we noticed that ah ... the hair of Leanne had been dyed and it is dyed a burgundy colour. Right, and as a result of noticing that burgundy colour in her hair, we returned to Alice Street that afternoon and we took possession of a bag from a rubbish bin in the back yard – which con ... it was a white plastic bag – it contained a number of items – toiletry items – razors, toothpaste, shower hooks.

Stafford: Can I step in? Fynes-Clinton: Yes.

Stafford: When she left on the Monday, she had white hair – she hadn't done anything to her hair and I'll swear on a hundred bibles her hair had definitely not been dyed.

Fynes-Clinton: All right.

Stafford: And the dye in question wasn't a burgundy anyway, it was a streaking kit which is blonde.

Fynes-Clinton: All right, well I'm just stating to you here Graham, as a result of what we thought was dyed hair on the body, right, we went back to the house at Goodna there and we located this plastic bag with these toiletry items in it – toothpaste, there was shower hooks from a curtain or something, in there – are you aware of that bag at all.

Stafford: I'm not aware of the bag, but the shower curtain is new.

Fynes-Clinton: Yes. When you say the shower curtain is new, which one are you talking about?

Stafford: The one that's in there now. Three or four weeks.

Fynes-Clinton: And who put it there?

Stafford: Melissa.

Fynes-Clinton: Melissa.

Stafford: The old one had all mildew on the bottom so we threw it out …

Later, Detective Senior Constable Fynes-Clinton continued to question Graham about the blood found on items in the boot and glove box of his car and about the tyre tracks found at the body site:

Fynes-Clinton: All right. Now, tests have been conducted in the laboratories in Brisbane and ah doctors in there, ah the chemists have told us that the blood on a canvas bag in your boot, blood on a blanket from the boot of your car, blood found in the bathroom of the house up there and blood of the body of Leanne Holland is of the same grouping. Do you wish to make any comment about that?

Graham: What can I say? You tell me – I don't believe it. I know it wasn't me. What can I say?

Fynes-Clinton: There was also a stay-sharp knife located in the … ah … glove box of the Gemini, and they also tell us that had traces of blood on it.

Graham: (shakes head) …

Fynes-Clinton: Okay, so at now in relation to where the body of Leanne was located out the bushland at Redbank Plains, there was some tyre tracks … located there, next to the body, as I said the scientific people have taken photographs and tests on those tyre tracks and they're able to tell us – that are on your car that we took possession of – match those to the ones out there at the scene. Can you comment on that at all?

Graham: I'd like to see some proof. I don't believe it. I honestly don't.

Fynes-Clinton: … so, even though the scientific people have told us about the blood and the tyres there, you can't help us …

Graham: I wish I could – I honestly wish I could. If you think I could so something like that, you're sadly mistaken. Fynes-Clinton: Do something like what?

Graham: Murder somebody – I mean, it's just not something I would do.

Fynes-Clinton: … now, in relation to the stay-sharp knife in your glove box, were you aware that that was there?

Graham: I had forgotten, but it has been for quite some time.

Fynes-Clinton: And … where is that knife from?

Graham: I think it was in the car when I bought it. I just happened to find it and throw it in the glove box … There's no reason for it, I mean I probably should have thrown it away.

Later in the interview Detective Senior Constable Fynes-Clinton asked Graham whether he had cleaned the interior of his car boot and again implied that the scientific officers indicated that the boot had been cleaned. Graham emphatically denied cleaning it and indeed claimed he had never cleaned the inside of his boot. He merely noted that:

'When I lived at Mum's there was always like a vacuum cleaner that enables me to clean it easily, same as when I lived at Arthur's, but since we've lived at Melissa's dad's there just hasn't been the facilities and it just hasn't been done. It hasn't been cleaned. Last time it was even cleaned inside … it was on a Sunday a few weeks ago, as I say, Melissa did a little bit of cleaning when I was sick. She cleaned up the upholstery … '

Fynes-Clinton continued his line of questioning asking Graham who had cleaned the house. Specifically he wondered whether anyone had mopped the upstairs, and indicated to Graham that scientific tests suggested that the floors had been cleaned:

Fynes-Clinton: Do you do any wiping or mopping at all?

Graham: No mopping. Maybe a little bit of wiping, in the kitchen.

Fynes-Clinton: And … ah, well who does it? Who does the mopping?

Graham: Melissa.

Fynes-Clinton: Does Leanne do the mopping?

Graham: She might have, I can't recall …

Fynes-Clinton: On Monday morning, do you agree that previously you've told us … after Leanne had left the house, you received a phone call from Patricia Lynch?

Graham: That's correct.

Fynes-Clinton: And ah, just again, the basis of your conversation sort of with her was, can you just reiterate what that is again, thanks.

Graham: She asked me if Leanne was there and I said 'no she's gone down the shops', and, to the best of my knowledge, I'm pretty sure she said well, she was going down there …

Fynes-Clinton: We've … ah, taken a statement from Trisha and she's informed us that she said to you after you told her that Leanne had gone down to the shops for you to … when Leanne comes back, to tell her to come down to the caravan park and see her down there. Do you recall that at all?

Graham: No – definitely not.

Fynes-Clinton: Are you sure that she never said that …

Graham: Positive.

11

True lies

As the interview continued Detective Richards joined the questioning, asking Graham about his earlier statement and some discrepancies within it.

Richards: ... after this, later in the day we find out that there's different movements that you've made that you didn't tell me about earlier in the morning ...

Graham: The visit to the Plaza I happened to forget about, but ... um.

Richards: You also forgot about the visit to the car wash. Fynes-Clinton: And you also forgot about the visit to the doctor's on the Tuesday, not the Monday.

Graham: No, I knew it was on the Tuesday.

Richards: Well, why did you state to me ...

Graham: Because, every time ...

Richards: ... it was on the Monday.

Graham: Every five minutes you go back from Monday to Tuesday, and it confused me. I mean, that's only normal isn't it. Sorry.

Richards: In the statement, when we spoke to you about it, we were concentrating on your movements on Monday, we didn't worry about Tuesday. I asked you specifically in the beginning of the statement what were your movements on Monday.

Graham: Oh well anyway, you know whether I went to the doctor on Tuesday ... And I don't deny going to the doctor on Tuesday.

Richards: Now, do you agree that in all the statements you've given us, like the first statement on Mon ... on Wednesday, and the interview on Thursday ... That your story has changed considerably from the first statement you gave to the last one?

Graham: I wouldn't agree with that. I've just stated there are discrepancies. Sure. I'm confused.

Richards: And then also today there's ... further discrepancies in times that you've rung Melissa or that ... Terry's rung you. Do you agree with that?

Graham: I'd agree with it yeah.

Richards: Now is there any reason for it at all.

Graham: Only that I didn't make a note of what times everything happened. I mean I wish I had. Um, you know, there's no reason for it. On a normal day, I ring Melissa and she rings me – a couple of times. There's no big deal about it.

At this stage, Richards raised the issue of the maggot for the first time, asking Graham to explain why one was allegedly found in the boot of his car. Fynes-Clinton even offered him a plausible explanation by asking whether he ever went to the dump with rubbish.

Here, Graham demonstrated his naïveté. He had been given an opportunity to explain away the maggot in the boot. All he had to do was say that he had indeed, at some time, had rotting food in the boot. It would have been up to the police to prove otherwise. Instead he told them that he hadn't been to the dump for months. Richards continued his questioning:

Richards: And the size of the maggot coincided with the sizes of the maggots located on the body of ... Leanne Holland?

Graham: No.

Richards: When she was located.

Graham: No.

Richards: No idea how that maggot got there?

Graham: No. I don't believe it.

Richards: Well, I was there when the maggot was located, so you can't explain how come a maggot is present in the boot of your car?

Graham: No.

Fynes-Clinton: And you can't explain how the blood, that the people in town told us was located in your car got there?

Graham: Nah.

Fynes-Clinton: And you can't explain ... that there maybe similarities in your tyre tread out at the scene where the body was found?

Graham: No.

Richards: And you can't explain how that ... blood which was located ... in the boot of your car has been grouped to the blood of the body of Leanne Sarah Holland?

Graham: No.

A strong part of the police case was that Graham had lied at various times. They said, for instance, that he lied about attending the doctor's surgery on the Monday instead of the Tuesday and about injuring himself while changing the shock absorber on his car, when they alleged he injured himself bashing Leanne. They also said he lied about the amount of time he spent at Arthur Power's place. The judge, on summing up at the trial, raised the issue of Graham's truthfulness. He told the jury that the Crown was trying to show that by lying he was filling in his Monday afternoon to give himself an alibi. Stafford claimed he was not lying, but was confused by the police questioning.

By Saturday afternoon, after several days of police interrogation, it is apparent he was very confused. An extract from the interview reveals he was not alone in being confused – but it appears he was the only one assumed to be lying.

Richards: Right, Graham, do you agree that yesterday, when we spoke to you, we went over times that you'd stated in your original statement you gave to us on Tuesday – on Wednesday, sorry?

Graham: Yeah.

Richards: Do you agree that as we went through those times there was certain discrepancies in the times that you've stated and also different places where you've actually been, ah … in the statement?

Graham: There's a couple, yeah.

Richards: Right, now, ah, do you agree that in your original statement you stated to us that, ah … you arrived home at approximately 2.30 to 3 o'clock on the Wednesday – that was in your original statement?

Graham: On the Wednesday?

Richards: Sorry, on the Tuesday – on the Monday! You arrive back from Arthur Power's place to Goodna here. That time.

Graham: Yeah.

Richards: Then you worked on the car?

Graham: That's right.

Richards: That's when the injury occurred to your arm?

Graham: Yes.

Richards: And, ah, do you agree that in that statement you stated you attended a doctor on that afternoon?

Graham: Um. I'm not sure that I said that in my statement. If I did that was incorrect.

Richards: Do you agree that as a result of that interview yesterday it was clarified that you in fact had gone …

Graham: On the Tuesday?

Richards: On the Tuesday?

Graham: Yes.

Richards: Now, ah, do you agree that yesterday you did go to the car wash?

Graham: On Wednesday?

Richards: Beg pardon?

Graham: I wasn't here yesterday.

Richards: Sorry, on the Wednesday, yes.

Graham: Um. I went to the car wash, yeah.

Richards: And you went to the car wash after you'd come back from Arthur Power's place and worked on your car?

Graham: That's what I said, but I realise that was incorrect as well.

Richards: Now ah, what is your story from where you went from the car wash?

Graham: The car wash was Tuesday. It wasn't Monday. I remember now, because, ah ...

Fynes-Clinton: The car wash was Tuesday?

Graham: Let me think.

Fynes-Clinton: No, no, no – Monday was your day off, right?

Graham: Yeah.

Fynes-Clinton: And you went to work, Tuesday, didn't you?

Graham: Yes.

Fynes-Clinton: All right, and ah, I think well, Monday – the day off. That was the day you went to the car wash, wasn't it? As you recollect?

Graham: I'm not sure anymore, actually I'm starting to get so confused.

Richards: Do you agree that ...

Graham: I know it's something I can't hide because I've got a receipt – docket as you know, I mean ...

Quite obviously, Graham was not the only one confused about times and days. The police had not interviewed him 'yesterday' as was said so many times throughout this questioning, but in fact on the Thursday, two days earlier.

Did Graham Stafford lie to the police? Based on the evidence presented to the court, he did not. It was a crucial part of the Crown case that he did, but it is quite apparent from the interviews with the investigators, that all parties were confused, rather than lying.

To this day Terry Holland will not discuss the matter other than to say he believes Graham Stafford murdered his daughter because Stafford told him lies as to the whereabouts of Leanne on that first night she was missing.

He has been asked on many occasions by journalists to expand on that comment, but he refuses. It would appear he has no further evidence of lies other than the evidence that he gave to the court.

The same day, on Saturday 28 September, Graham was formally charged with the murder of Leanne Sarah Holland. He still did not have legal representation.

Even after his arrest, he continued to cooperate with the police. Two days later he signed a consent form allowing a government doctor to take samples of his blood, head and pubic hair and fingernail clippings to be compared with specimens obtained from Leanne's body. Despite being warned that he was not obliged to allow these samples to be taken and that any results could produce evidence against him, Graham believed cooperation was the best way to prove his innocence.

Graham Stafford appeared in the Ipswich Magistrates Court on Monday 30 September 1991, charged with the murder of Leanne Sarah Holland.

The courthouse was something of a circus. Police were there in force for the suspect's protection from the local community. It seemed the media had sent every reporter, photographer and television cameraperson available. It was a story tailor-made for newspapers and television – a young girl killed and mutilated, apparently by her sister's boyfriend.

As fate would have it, the media and public were directed to the wrong courtroom and Graham's appearance went largely unnoticed. Graham had no chance of being released on bail given the charge of murder and he was remanded until 2 December, when a magistrate would decide whether there was sufficient evidence to commit him for trial in the Supreme Court.

The police investigation did not stop with Graham's arrest. In early October 1991, 25 personnel searched bushland around where Leanne's body was found. The group included Goodna detectives,

State Emergency Service personnel and Queensland Police Academy cadets. A police spokesman described the search as 'part of routine police procedure in murder investigations'.

Clearly, while the police were convinced that Graham had committed the murder, they also recognised that the evidence they had was largely circumstantial. It appears they were looking for something more substantial.

12

First taste of prison

Graham's mother Jean later recounted those hours in the lead-up to her son's arrest:

Graham and Melissa had stayed the night at Arthur's house at Collingwood Park. They couldn't bear to stay any longer at Terry's house, with the constant memories of Leanne. They needed space and, to complicate matters, the police had seized all the bedding from the house for scientific testing, making sleeping there difficult. Terry chose to remain at the house and Melissa kept in constant contact with him and visited him daily. Terry, Melissa and Graham had not worked since the previous Wednesday.

Saturday morning we were up early, I don't think anyone had got much sleep. Graham was worried, not eating or sleeping much, but always sure everything would turn out okay because he had done the right thing by being honest and cooperative. My husband Eric, Graham and I sat on the back patio, we saw a policeman standing on a vacant lot at the back of the house watching us. There was also a surveillance van parked across the road opposite the house, at least, that is what it looked like.

Graham and Melissa told us all that had happened, what

the police had said and done. Melissa was very supportive of Graham. She hardly left his side the whole time we were there except to visit her father a few times to see what was going on. She said police showed them supposed specks of blood, which they could hardly see and she scoffed at them because they were so small and insignificant. They also said there was blood on the mop and that the house had been washed to which she replied: 'The mop and bucket have been on the back steps for the past two weeks with the same water in it.' The police really grilled them about there being a new shower curtain in the bathroom. Terry, Melissa and Graham all told them it had been there about two weeks. The old one had been taken away in the wheelie bin as it was mildewed. Graham said the tiles on the bathroom floor were loose and water was going through the floor. Terry lived underneath and told them they had better get a new curtain. The police took the tiles away.

The police said Leanne's hair had been dyed and they had found a hair dye box in the bin. Melissa said it was a box she had used when she had done her own hair, but she didn't think they believed her. Before finding Leanne the police had dug holes in their garden looking for her. Melissa and Graham were also trying to think how blood could possibly be on Graham's car, as the police had told him there was blood on his steering wheel, dashboard and car door that had been wiped clean. The police told them there was also blood on his hammer.

Eric and I were desperately thinking what we should do. We did not know any solicitors, as we never had need for them except when buying a house. Then I thought about the solicitor who we used when buying our house. She had told me that her husband was a criminal lawyer. We phoned them up. I told him what the situation was and he said, 'Tell him to cooperate with the police and if he is not guilty he has nothing to worry about.' We wanted to believe this was true so this is what we told Graham to do. It was what he had been doing anyway.

I smoked cigarettes almost continuously. Someone suggested

we play cards to give our minds a rest, because by this time we were going around in circles. We tried to play cards, but we could not concentrate so after about half an hour we gave up. We could not believe what was happening and we were sure the police would find the people who did this, then we could put this behind us, stop thinking about ourselves and grieve for Leanne and empathise with her family. Because of what was happening we had to put aside our feelings for Leanne.

To give you some idea of what happens to the human body at times like this, I lost three stone, which is almost twenty kilos of weight, in three weeks. Eric had bad chest pains, which we thought was a heart attack, and Stacey (Graham's sister) also lost weight and cried all the time. Graham also had chest pains and goodness only knows what else. He would not want us to worry anymore than we had to by letting us know if he felt ill.

At this time on the Saturday morning we were still hopeful of the police telling us they had found the killers. Little did we know they were not looking anywhere else; if they found anything which did not fit in with Graham being the murderer they disregarded the information. They did not seem to want to know.

About 10 a.m. we made sandwiches, which no one wanted, but we made ourselves eat. Melissa had been to see her father again and told us what had been happening at his place. The waiting was terrible. The only incident I could compare it was with the 1974 Brisbane floods when we could see all the devastation and were waiting to see what would happen next, would it get better or would it get worse? But this time it was much more personal, much more devastating and a hundred times worse.

I don't remember the exact time, but sometime in the afternoon the police arrived in two cars, at least four policemen, maybe more, there seemed to be a house full of them. We had been talking about asking the police if Graham could go home with us for the weekend, they probably heard this in their surveillance van. Melissa had just got back from seeing her father when they knocked and just walked in. They asked Graham and Melissa to go to the Goodna Police Station to answer more questions.

We followed in our car and waited in the front office. Melissa said the policeman who had interrogated her had been very nasty. He had insinuated she had been an accomplice. She waited in the foyer with us and was in tears. She said the policeman had told her Graham was guilty, they had found the blood in the car and on the steering wheel, dashboard, in the boot, on a hammer and on a bag. There was also a knife in the glove box and tyre tracks like his at the scene.

They told her there was a four-hour gap in Graham's story about what he did on the Monday. The police said Graham had made too many mistakes and he had lied. The only thing they didn't have was someone seeing him do it.

They also told her all the gory details of what happened to her sister. She had been sodomised through a hole in her pants, her face had been battered and her hair had been dyed. This had all been done so no one would recognise her. She told us this in the police waiting room where we sat for about five minutes crying in each other's arms. This was the only time she had cried in front of us from the Friday morning when we arrived. She is a very strong girl. She still didn't believe Graham had done it, but she said she dared not go and see him, as they would implicate her in the crime. She told me when I saw him that night we should tell him she would still wear his ring and his chain and still believed in him.

The police came out sometime later and said they had just charged Graham, and asked if we wanted to see him before he was put in the watch house at Ipswich. Graham was very upset and looked like he was in shock. We tried to reassure him, and told him we would get a solicitor. It was a terrible time for everyone concerned. I can only guess how Graham felt, or Eric or Stacey. I could see how they looked and I never want to see that look again. I phoned the solicitor who sounded surprised, he said, 'But the blood analysis tests won't be back until Monday so why did they not wait until then?' He was also shocked at the amount of interview tapes that had been done. After charging Graham, a policeman tried to convince us Graham was guilty by saying they had found tracks with different tyres at the scene and Graham's car had different tyres. Also there was a maggot in Graham's boot similar to that found at the scene. There was blood on a hammer and there was a knife in the glove box. He also said there had been blood in the house and that it had been cleaned up.

The rest of that day was a nightmare and we have been living a nightmare ever since and will continue to do so until Graham comes home. Later that night Melissa phoned us to see how he was. I told her the first question Graham asked when we went to see him was 'Where's Melissa?' I said: 'She is okay, think about yourself,' but he said, 'No she's not, look after her, Mum.'

Melissa's father eventually took her to see a solicitor who told her not to see or contact Graham or his family again. After leaving us a letter at Arthur Power's place, this is exactly what she did. I don't blame her for doing this at this terrible time. She said someone could collect Graham's clothes and personal things from the house. Everything which belonged to Graham before they met, but the things they bought between them such as the television, video recorder, washing machine, etc she was keeping. The next day when I spoke with her on the telephone she asked me to pass on a message to Graham: 'Tell him I still don't think he did it, my father doesn't either, but he is keeping an open mind.'

That first weekend in custody, Graham shared a cell with a person he believes was a police informant; the same person he believes provided the information which became Item 25 on the police running sheet.

The police still did not have a confession as Graham continued to deny any involvement in Leanne's death.

Despite constant questions, Graham made no admissions to his cellmate. Graham believes that this was a man who has since been convicted of incest against his two daughters and is serving a long prison sentence. Item 25 of the police running sheet reads:

> Information from informant known to this office that missing person is a former resident of Baillee Street and was widely regarded by locals as a young girl who roamed the street and had a nickname of H.J. (standing for head job) and she was said to perform oral sex on young local youths for monetary reward. Also says that her father is a drunk and that the child went mostly unsupervised.

Throughout his investigations for the Stafford family Graeme Crowley was unable to determine whether the person who supplied this information about Leanne to the police was the same man who shared Graham's prison cell that first weekend and who was later convicted of incest.

In 1996 Crowley interviewed the two daughters of the man believed to have been the man in the cell with Graham. The women, both in their twenties, were interviewed in the presence of their mother. Crowley was informed the father had been sentenced to a lengthy prison sentence for the abuse of his daughters. They claimed they had not complained about their father until after they moved out of the family home because they feared for their lives.

After his conviction the man told them and their mother that he will kill them all on his release from prison. The women claimed that on a number of occasions he had shown them photographs of Leanne taken after her death, highlighting her injuries.

He threatened that they would 'end up like her' if they said anything about what he did to them. They also told Crowley one of his favourite pastimes was to burn them with cigarettes and cigarette lighters. The man called them 'smilies' because the disposable lighters left a burn on the skin similar to a smile.

The daughters also told Crowley that in the past their father had taken both of them to the bush track where Leanne's body was found for sex. One daughter is permanently deaf in one ear from the constant back-handers she received from her father, the women told Crowley.

The daughters told Crowley that when they lived with their father, detectives were constantly at the house drinking with him. For this reason, they felt they could not trust the police enough to tell them what their father was doing to them. They alleged he has a lengthy criminal history spanning many years.

They recounted that during the investigation into Leanne's murder, they heard discussions between their father and investigators. They felt he was leading the investigation, bizarre as it sounds, telling the police what inquiries they should be making and where they should be looking. They also claimed he was at the bush track where Leanne's body was discovered, when police were removing the body. They had seen him on the nightly news coverage of the investigation.

In 2003 a prison inmate came forwards, informing prison authorities that he believed his cellmate was responsible for the murder of Leanne Holland. It came as a surprise to all involved when it was established this was the same person Stafford suspected, the man who had shared his cell after his arrest.

The inmate made a number of allegations, including the claim that this prisoner was obsessed with the murder and continually spoke of it. He claimed that the prisoner in question had photographs of the deceased in the condition in which she was found. He was told to keep his mouth shut and return to his cell.

His family approached investigative journalist Darrell Giles with the information. They told Giles that the prisoner in question, during the course of his seven-year sentence for rape and incest, spent many weekends out of jail on leave, courtesy of police. In fact, he bragged about it.

Giles was able to confirm independently that, during one seven-month period alone, the prisoner was given the equivalent of every second weekend on leave, apparently at the request of police. Giles sought permission from the corrective services department to interview the informant, but his request was declined. Giles published the story based on the information from the inmate's family and his own investigations. He must wait until this prisoner is released before he can obtain the full story. Giles broke the story in *The Sunday Mail* on 30 April 2006:

> A violent sex offender – named as a suspect in the Leanne Holland murder case and a known police informant – was repeatedly given weekend leave from his prison cell. He was often seen in the company of police detective acquaintances. He is alleged to have boasted to other prisoners of being let out to go drinking and have sex. The offender was the same man named by two sisters in *The Sunday Mail* report last year as being responsible for 12-year-old Leanne Holland's brutal murder in 1991.

The then opposition leader Lawrence Springborg raised the matter in Parliament and called for an immediate inquiry, however, nothing further was done. Giles has applied under Freedom of Information Legislation for full details of all leave dates of this prisoner. As yet that information has not been made available to him. On 2 July 2006 Darrell Giles wrote a further article for *The Sunday Mail*.

> A violent sex offender, recently named as a suspect in the Leanne Holland murder case, freely mingled with police at the bushland spot where the schoolgirl's body was found. In a startling new development to the long-running case, a source has come forward after seeing the 1991 film of the crime scene replayed on Channel 7. The source said the film showed the man talking to detectives behind crime scene tape at Redbank Plains soon after police had found the Ipswich schoolgirl's bashed and partially naked body. Sources said the man – a police informant – was taken to the scene by detectives and also accompanied them to the Holland house in Goodna,

where she was allegedly killed. The informant, now 52, also claimed to have worked 'undercover' for police on the case and helped secure the conviction of Graham Stafford.

Most of this information has circulated as rumour for some years, but these recent developments indicate that this is perhaps more than rumour. The allegations at least warrant attention by a police oversight body such as the Crime and Misconduct Commission. This prisoner, however, is not the only suspicious character in this case.

Above: Graham Stafford celebrates his birthday before the disappearance and murder of his girlfriend's younger sister, Leanne Holland.

Graeme Crowley

Above: The pedestrian bridge and the Ipswich motorway next to the caravan park in Goodna, home to Leanne's friend Trisha Lynch.

Below: Leanne's father holding her photo shortly after the discovery of her body. (September 1991, *The Courier-Mail*)

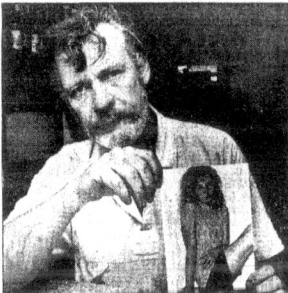

TERRY Holland with a picture of his murdered daughter, Leanne.

Young girl bashed to death

By JULIAN BURKE

GOODNA schoolgirl Leanne Holland was horribly bashed to death with a hammer or similar blunt object a post-mortem examination revealed yesterday.

The 12-year-old girl's injuries to the head and upper body were so extensive police had to rely on fingerprints to identify the body.

The body was decomposing after three days dumped in scrub at Redbank Plains, which also hampered identification.

Investigation co-ordinator Det Insp Wayne King described the callous killer as "certainly not the full quid".

"She was pretty badly assaulted around the head and upper body region," he said.

He refused to reveal if Leanne had been sexually assaulted and the nature of "other injuries" she suffered.

Her battered and partly naked body was found on Thursday between two tracks about 30m from busy Redbank Plains Rd.

Leanne was last seen alive about 9.30am on Monday when she set out for shops just 500m from her family home in Alice St.

Grieving father Terry Holland, a single parent, was being comforted yesterday by counsellors from the Victims of Crime association.

"The family are having a pretty rough time at the moment," Insp King said.

The killer made no attempt to conceal the body which was discovered by two police trail bike riders investigating a report of a suspicious car in the area.

"Any murder is gruesome but the fact that it is a 12-year-old child makes it 10 times as bad," Insp King said.

He said investigators were waiting for the results of forensic tests, expected on Monday, for new leads into the death.

Insp King would not reveal if current leads included a bloodstained car found in the Goodna area.

He described the public response as excellent and appealed for anyone with information to contact Goodna police on 288 2999.

Above: The Cecil Hotel and, across the road, 70a Alice Street – the home shared by the Hollands and Graham Stafford.

Below: The Goodna shopping centre looking towards Alice Street.

Graham Stafford's car, showing the distinctive O'Neill sticker.

Above: Stafford family and friends at Moreton Correctional Centre at a family day barbecue.

Below: Parents and friends with Graham at Palen Creek a couple of years before his release.

Graeme Crowley and television presenter Carmel Travers compare impressions from the crime scene with transparencies from Stafford's car.

Graeme Crowley

Above: The Stafford family at a friend's wedding, just after Graham's release.

Below: *The Sunday Mail*'s February 1997 article with Leanne's photo.

Book reveals sisters' sensational murder evidence

Our dad killed Leanne

EXCLUSIVE

By DARRELL GILES

TWO sisters have claimed their father was responsible for a shocking sex murder, despite another man being jailed for life.

They say their father – a violent convicted sex offender – was the man who tortured and killed Goodna schoolgirl Leanne Holland in 1991, not her brother-in-law Graham Stafford.

Stafford has always strenuously denied he killed the 12-year-old and family and supporters have campaigned to have him freed.

The sensational new claims are contained in a book by former detective Graeme Crowley and criminologist Paul Wilson. Who

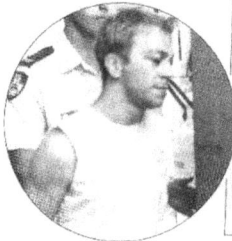

MYSTERY: Graham Stafford *(far left)*, and murdered sister-in-law Leanne Holland

BRUTAL: Police at Redbank Plains bushland after Leanne Holland's body was discovered

Suspect at murder site

New twist in Leanne Holland case

By DARRELL GILES
political editor

A VIOLENT sex offender, recently named as a suspect in the Leanne Holland murder case, mingled freely with police at the bushland spot where the schoolgirl's body was found.

In a startling new development to the long-running case, a source has come forward after seeing 1991 film of the crime scene replayed on Channel 7.

The source said the film showed the man talking to detectives behind crime scene tape at Redbank Plains soon after police had found the Ipswich schoolgirl's bashed and partially naked body.

Sources said the man — a police informant — was taken to the scene by detectives and also accompanied them to the Holland house in Goodna, where she was allegedly killed.

The informant, now 52, also claimed later to have worked "undercover" for police on the case and helped secure the conviction of Graham Stafford.

Stafford, 42, was paroled in May after serving four months short of 15 years in jail for the sex slaying of his then-fiancee's sister. He has always strenuously denied killing Leanne, 12.

His supporters, who are working on a legal petition to have Stafford pardoned, were shocked to discover the other man's involvement in the case.

The man was in the same jail as Stafford after being convicted of rape and incest in 1996 and serving a full seven-year sentence.

The Sunday Mail revealed in April that the man was repeatedly given weekend leave from prison and was often seen in the company of plainclothes police.

He was the same man named by two sisters last year as being linked to the Holland murder. They said their claims were never investigated by police.

In the 2005 book *Who Killed Leanne?* by Graeme Crowley and Paul Wilson, the sisters revealed:
● Their father knew Leanne and had raped the sisters at the same bushland.
● He had tortured them, leaving similar cigarette lighter burns as found on Leanne.
● He had photos of her corpse which he had either taken himself or had come from the official police file, and threatened the sisters that they would end up like Leanne if they talked.

Above: An article in 2006 in *The Sunday Mail,* reporting on another suspect in the case and his links to the crime scene.

13

He did not do it

Before Graham's committal hearing came around, there was to be another nightmare in Goodna. Less than three weeks after the people of Goodna were confronted with the horror of Leanne's murder, the unthinkable happened. Another twelve-year-old girl, Julie-Ann Lowe, was molested and murdered barely a kilometre from Leanne's home.

At around 7.30 a.m. on Tuesday 16 October 1991, Julie-Ann was walking from her home to the Goodna Railway Station to catch a train to school. As was her usual fashion, she walked alongside the Ipswich Motorway, past the Goodna Caravan Park and down, under the bridge over Woogaroo Creek – the same path Leanne often used when visiting her friends in the caravan park.

Julie-Ann was accosted, sexually molested and drowned. Her body was left in Woogaroo Creek, less than 100 metres from the camping area of the Goodna Caravan Park.

Police sped to the scene and sealed off the area. They knew for certain Graham Stafford did not commit this murder – he was in prison. They questioned the caravan park residents and several told police they had seen a park resident, eighteen-year-old Sean McPhedran running from the direction of the creek, his clothes dripping wet. He was arrested and charged with her murder. Bail was refused.

Considered too mentally ill to plead to the charge, McPhedran was incarcerated in the nearby Wolston Park Hospital. Upon reassessment almost two years later, he was tried and found guilty of Julie-Ann's murder.

When Graham Stafford's charge eventually came to trial, his defence counsel raised the circumstances surrounding Julie-Ann's murder. The prosecution objected, arguing that Leanne had been bashed to death whereas Julie-Ann Lowe was drowned. The Crown argued that, because the means of death were different, the two crimes were not connected. The Crown further claimed that because McPhedran could not drive, he could not be involved in Leanne's murder, as her body had been transported almost ten kilometres from Goodna.

Eric and Jean Stafford had suspicions about Sean McPhedran. They could not accept that there were two unconnected murders of twelve-year-old girls so close together in time and place. Police claimed that McPhedran did not know Leanne and that he was not living at the caravan park at the time of her murder. Records obtained by Crowley from the caravan park in 1993, however, showed McPhedran did live at the caravan park when Leanne was killed. A photocopy of the park register confirmed he had moved into the park on 3 September. A notation on the register indicated the original had been handed to police.

When Crowley spoke to Trisha Lynch in Sydney, she said that Sean McPhedran not only knew Leanne, but that she had introduced them to each other. McPhedran's mother was also aware that her son knew Leanne. Crowley's inquiries with McPhedran's employer at the Redbank Plaza Shopping Centre, where the young man worked as a trolley collector, revealed that McPhedran did not turn up for work on the Monday and Tuesday of Leanne's disappearance. Normally, he was most punctual and rarely missed a day's work.

McPhedran's mother was very cooperative towards Crowley, despite knowing his suspicions about her son's possible role in Leanne's murder, even to the point of permitting a search of her car for evidence. She told Crowley that her son could drive a car, even though he didn't have a licence, and that she allowed him to drive it. In fact, he had driven the car from Goodna to Toowong Cemetery one night and collided with a tombstone. Yet, the police had always claimed that he could not drive a car. McPhedran's mother made an interesting comment to Crowley during one of their meetings at her house:

> I have wondered myself whether Sean has any knowledge of Leanne's death. I have wondered if, perhaps, he witnessed her death and then killed Julie-Ann to copy what they did.

Mrs McPhedran confirmed that her son knew Leanne and that he had played football with her at the caravan park. She also told Crowley that when Sean was aged five, he was in the bath with his three-year-old brother when his brother drowned and she was convinced that Sean was 'involved'.

His mother also admitted that when McPhedran was six he tried to strangle a girl in the school classroom. Crowley traced the mother of this child who told him:

> I used to collect my daughter every afternoon after school. I was sitting at the front gate and when after ten minutes she didn't arrive I walked down to the classroom. McPhedran was behind her with his hands around her throat. Three or four other children were trying to pull him off her. She was starting to go blue in the face. I raced over to where they were and it took all my strength to force him to let go. At that time the teacher arrived because some of the children had raced away to summon help. We revived my daughter. She wasn't unconscious, but was very groggy and couldn't talk for a few minutes.
>
> McPhedran attacked her out of the blue for no reason. The teacher took me aside and apologised. He admitted that he had been told not to leave McPhedran alone in the classroom with the other children. He promised there would not be a repeat occurrence where Sean was left alone, and asked me to keep the

incident to myself. The teacher explained that Sean's mother had told the teaching staff that she believed Sean might have been involved in the drowning of his brother.

After that, I removed my daughter from the class. Some time later, I started working in the tuckshop and McPhedran's mother apologised to me about the incident. She repeated the story about the drowning and said to me: 'I think he did it'. Mrs McPhedran told the police, but no one seemed interested, according to her.

According to his mother, at the age of sixteen, McPhedran also tried to strangle his twelve-year-old brother. It was this continual violent and bizarre behaviour that forced his mother to turn him out of the house. His sister also told Crowley in 1993 that McPhedran tried to kill her by holding her down and forcing her to swallow an overdose of sleeping tablets. The girl was taken to the Ipswich Hospital, where she had her stomach pumped.

Prior to being kicked out of home, McPhedran had been interested in the occult and had attended séances. He had also visited cemeteries at night with friends. Acquaintances of his confirmed the séance sessions. His mother stated she had been to every government agency available to try and get help for her son. She claimed her requests were repeatedly turned down or ignored, although Sean had spent some time in a home.

After Crowley's disastrous visit to detectives in 1993 with his concerns of a miscarriage of justice, he again visited McPhedran's mother. Her very hostile husband met him at the door. Police had visited them, he said, and both he and his wife thought that Crowley was spreading lies about Sean. The police told them not to talk to Crowley and they were following their advice. This was the end of any cooperation from the McPhedran family.

In June 1993, Crowley made inquiries as to the whereabouts of Sean McPhedran with a view to visiting him. He wasn't sure such a visit would achieve anything, but he felt he should talk to him face-to-face. McPhedran had never been questioned about Leanne's death and perhaps it was time he was asked if he knew anything about it. Crowley telephoned Wolston Park mental hospital and asked if Sean McPhedran was a patient. He was put on hold before being transferred to a ward. He again asked if McPhedran was a patient and was again put on hold. Then, a male voice came on the line:

'Hello,' the man said.
'Can you tell me if Sean McPhedran is an inmate there please?' Crowley asked.
The man replied: 'This is Sean.'
Taken aback, Crowley asked: 'Sean McPhedran?'
'Yes,' the man said.

He told McPhedran who he was and that he was making inquiries into the murder of Leanne Holland, then asked him: 'Sean, were you involved in Leanne's murder?'

McPhedran said: 'No, I did not know her. I was charged with the murder of Julie-Ann Lowe.' McPhedran went on to tell Crowley that he did not know Trisha Lynch and again stated that he did not know Leanne Holland and that he 'didn't mix with anyone'.

McPhedran suffered chronic psychotic schizophrenia. The symptoms included talking to himself, a morbid fascination with bizarre ideas, social isolation and poor personal hygiene. He slept with a knife under his pillow. According to his mother, this was because he apparently feared the devil would cut him open and drink his blood for not doing as he was told. He was fascinated by witchcraft, she said, and had visited cemeteries.

His mother gave sworn evidence that he had tried to commit suicide twice, read pornographic magazines and watched pornographic and violent movies. She said that while living at home he had to be forced to take a shower, usually after many days of not washing, and would use a towel as a substitute for toilet paper if none was available, throwing the towel on the floor afterwards.

The trial judge described the case as an indictment of a society that had failed to treat McPhedran. He commented that McPhedran should have received treatment well before he ever reached the stage of thinking about killing anyone. Although he pleaded not guilty to the murder charge on the grounds of unsoundness of mind, the prosecution called evidence to show that McPhedran had run away from the scene of the crime and had told lies to the police. He was convicted of murder.

In comparing the psychological profiles of Graham Stafford and Sean McPhedran, the differences could not be more apparent. Graham had a normal upbringing within a cooperative, supportive family and no apparent trauma in his life. There was also no evidence of dysfunctional behaviour in his past. He was not a social misfit and had no previous criminal convictions. During Graham's 28 years there had been no instances or warning signs of any erratic or antisocial behaviour. This profile was quite the opposite to that of McPhedran.

Curiously, one is reminded of the comment made by the police inspector in charge of the investigation into Leanne's murder that the killer 'was certainly not the full quid'. There is nothing in Graham's background, or in the evidence presented by police that would explain any sudden behavioural change resulting in him committing murder. To all who know him he is definitely 'the full quid'.

McPhedran was placed in the same prison as Graham. By this time, it was common knowledge within the general and prison community that Graham's family suspected McPhedran was perhaps involved somehow in Leanne's murder. The prison administration was concerned that Graham would try to harm McPhedran, blaming him for his incarceration.

Graham, however, calmly assured everyone this was not the case. He later said he would never show an act of violence to anyone, including McPhedran. Graham said he believes such an act would only confirm to the prison administration that he is capable of violence – a claim he denies. For some years, McPhedran and Graham lived harmoniously, side-by-side in the same prison. Graham Stafford has never attacked nor threatened him.

14

A hand up brief

As Graham's committal hearing approached, the Stafford family, who had no previous contact whatsoever with the law, learned much about the Australian judicial process.

Initially, they were dismayed to find that nothing happened overnight in the legal system.

After his arrest, they were told it would take two to three months before Graham could be arraigned in a lower court, where a magistrate would assess the evidence against him and decide whether he should be sent for trial. They were warned that Graham probably would be imprisoned for months before his name could be cleared at a trial. His parents and sister could not believe that Graham would have to suffer the indignity of imprisonment for so long before what they saw as a complete misunderstanding could be cleared up.

Prior to the committal hearing, it was explained to his family that it was common for all parties to the hearing to agree to the presentation of a 'hand up brief '. The brief is a collection of sworn statements obtained by the police from witnesses considered relevant to prove their charge.

It is usually the case that the brief does not contain statements from all witnesses interviewed by police, only those witnesses they feel are important to their side of the story. The brief is then passed to the Director of Public Prosecutions (DPP) who in turn hands a copy to the defence counsel and magistrate.

A defence counsel has the right to cross-examine any witnesses if he or she considers it necessary to negate the charge or clarify ambiguous aspects of it. It is usual for the defence to cross-examine some, but not every witness. This procedure saves the prosecution and defence an enormous amount of time and money. The downside, however, is that the defence counsel does not get to see all witnesses give their evidence and cannot test their claims until they appear at the subsequent trial before the judge and jury.

By the time Graham's committal hearing began, he had been in prison for more than two months. When it was found he could not afford a lawyer, Graham was granted legal aid and was represented by barrister Adrian Gundelach. Respected in Queensland legal circles as a very competent barrister specialising in criminal law, Mr Gundelach is known to seize tightly upon crucial aspects of the cases he handles.

In the Ipswich Magistrates Court on the morning of 2 December, Graham was formally charged with Leanne's murder. He was not asked at this stage to enter a plea to the charge. The DPP tendered 43 statements and nineteen exhibits that formed the basis of their case against him. Mr Gundelach chose to cross-examine only five witnesses. They were the arresting officer Fynes-Clinton, the police pathologist Dr Ashby, forensic science specialist Bill Crick, scientific analyst Kristine Bentley and police officer David Bennett. It was not therefore necessary for the other 38 witnesses to appear at that court hearing.

Detective Alan Fynes-Clinton was the first prosecution witness called. Mr Gundelach cut straight to the chase in his cross-examination. He questioned Fynes-Clinton about the colour of Leanne's hair at the time her body was found and canvassed Graham's part in the alleged dyeing of Leanne's hair.

In response to a series of probing questions from the barrister, Fynes-Clinton admitted that the police thought Leanne's hair had been dyed, despite Graham's continual denials to the contrary. This apparently is why they suspected he was lying. However, Fynes-

Clinton also conceded that scientific tests had proved conclusively that Leanne's hair had not been dyed before she was killed.

Tests had found that the distinctive red colouring through her hair, thought to be a hair dye, was unquestionably her own blood. As Leanne had received shocking head wounds, this was hardly surprising, but despite the early admission by the lead detective, the issue of Leanne's hair colour would haunt this case through the trial and even to the appeals court.

Mr Gundelach wasted no time in targeting other contentious issues with Fynes-Clinton. He broached the crucial area of Graham's clothing and the detective agreed the police had seized all they could find and sent it for scientific analysis. Fynes-Clinton admitted that no traces of blood, seminal fluid or other evidence was discovered on any of Graham's clothing.

Gundelach also asked about the new shower curtain that Melissa had installed. Police found the old curtain hooks in the rubbish bin, but no trace of the curtain. The detective agreed the police had canvassed the possibility of the old curtain being used to wrap Leanne's body before it was transported.

It was a theory with no basis, not supported by evidence and continually denied by Graham and the others in the household. While it could be seen as a red herring, it would come back to haunt him too.

Gundelach asked Fynes-Clinton what evidence the police relied upon in order to charge Graham with murder. Fynes-Clinton nominated 'the blood and the tyres'. When asked 'which blood?' he responded, 'Well, the boot, the house, yes … and the tyres. Two separate tread patterns matched up to two tyres on his car. There was the … he had opportunity on the 23rd and there were other things that have come out since.' Thus, Graham was arrested for murder based on small quantities of blood in the boot of his car and the house, matching tyre impressions and opportunity – plus other things that came out later. Curiously, the maggot did not rate a mention.

The next witness of note Mr Gundelach cross-examined was

forensic specialist Bill Crick. He told of his initial examination of Graham's Gemini sedan on Wednesday and its subsequent removal to police premises, where a more detailed scientific examination could be carried out.

An extract from Crick's diary dated and timed: '1200hrs 26 September', recorded that he received positive test results to haemoglobin on various parts of the inside and outside of the vehicle as well as to specific contents in the boot. These included a blanket, blue rag, green rag and a black and red tool bag. A knife and camera in the glove box and a seat cover also tested positive.

His diary does not record, however, taking possession of the maggot he saw in the boot on the previous day. Indeed, the only document to confirm that Crick had collected a maggot was a handwritten list of items he called an 'Exhibits List'.

> As well as being undated, the list appeared to be in no particular order, yet Crick said he compiled it as he examined the car. The sequence reflected in that list was: glove box, boot, boot, passenger floor, boot, boot, driver's door, passenger door, boot, boot, boot, boot, steering wheel, and finally boot.

Leanne's body was not found until the Thursday afternoon, yet documents exist for the Wednesday and Thursday morning in which Crick has recorded the offence being investigated variously as 'homicide' or 'murder'. The reasons for this were neither requested nor offered at the committal hearing nor Graham's subsequent trial.

It is noted that Crick later stated under oath that he was involved in no more than a missing person investigation. This begs the question of whether Crick and other investigating police had information that led them to begin a Major Incident Investigation immediately after Leanne was reported missing. Mr Gundelach savaged police witnesses at the committal hearing on this point.

Crick admitted that he made no written record on that day of finding the maggot. Given an opportunity to explain his belief about the investigation before Leanne's body was found and asked whether he was looking for a dead body, Crick said that at the time it was only a missing person investigation. In his cross-examination, Mr Gundelach zeroed in on critical points, including the tyre tracks found in dirt where Leanne's body was discovered. Crick said he believed the tracks to be the same as the treads on Stafford's Gemini.

Under further questioning, Crick disputed that Sangur tests were unreliable, but agreed the test strips reacted to vegetation and rust. It was apparent that Mr Gundelach had researched carefully in preparation for Graham's defence. He had Crick confirm that he had told other investigating police that he believed the boot of Graham's car had been wiped out. Crick reached this conclusion, he told the court, because the Sangur test gave a positive reaction, yet he could find no trace of blood in the boot.

The last witness called at the committal hearing was Senior Constable David Bennett of Townsville Police Station, who had calculated the time of Leanne's death from the growth rate and egg-laying time of maggots found on her body. Bennett said that he had identified all maggot specimens handed to him as *Lucilia cuprina*. He told the court that Crick had provided him with the maximum and minimum air temperatures for the Goodna neighbourhood for the period 23 to 26 September. Armed with these data, Bennett said he was able to calculate the approximate growth rate of the maggots and an egg-laying time. In his opinion, Leanne died sometime between mid-afternoon and midnight on Monday.

The prosecution requested a minor, but significant alteration to Bennett's statement – the temperatures obtained for the stated period were for the area of Ipswich and not Brisbane. It is commonly known in South East Queensland that temperatures at Ipswich vary to those on the coastal fringe according to the time of year.

The selective nature of the hand up brief practically ensured that Graham would be committed for trial. It did nevertheless give Gundelach and his team the brief against which they had to build a defence.

Graham entered a not guilty plea and was committed for trial in the Brisbane Supreme Court at the next sittings. Bail was refused and he went back to his prison cell. The DPP had its committal, but it was not without problems.

No motive had been established and the window of opportunity for Graham to have committed the crime was diminishing. Bennett's estimation of the time of death was less than satisfactory. The police had a lot of loose ends to tie up before the trial.

15

His day in court

By the time his eight-day trial began on Monday 16 March 1992, Graham Stafford had spent almost six months in prison. Mr Gundelach was involved in another criminal trial at the time and the Legal Aid Office had to appoint another barrister to represent him.

Luck, if it can be considered as having any part in the criminal justice system, was not running his way. Charles Clark took Graham's case on the Friday before the trial started, taking on the Herculean task of studying the evidence, statements and background to the case in a single weekend. Mr Clark had just two days to ensure he was equipped to mount the defence at the Supreme Court on Monday morning.

As is customary in criminal trials, the first procedure was the selection and empanelment of the jury under the watchful eye of the trial judge, Mr Justice Derrington. The prosecutor Mr Bullock named those witnesses he intended to call to prove the case against Graham. This gave the jurors an opportunity to speak up if they knew, or might be unduly influenced by, any potential witness.

The prosecution witnesses included the police involved in the case (Richards, Fynes-Clinton and Crick), as well as the members of Leanne's immediate family (Terry, Melissa and Craig), a range of citizens who claimed they had sighted Leanne or who had dealings with Graham Stafford on the day of her disappearance, plus forensic experts including Beryl Morris, Rosemary Ashby and Angela van Daal.

Mr Bullock opened the case against Graham with a lengthy address to the jury, in which he outlined the evidence of witnesses he contended proved beyond a reasonable doubt that Graham Stafford murdered Leanne Holland. He went through the blood and DNA evidence and the tyre tracks; but admitted to the jury he could not offer a motive for Graham to have committed the murder.

It is worth noting here that the question of motive is of more legal concern to investigators than to a prosecutor. To an investigator, finding a person with both the motive and opportunity to commit a crime is the first step towards identifying the perpetrator. There is no requirement in law however for the Crown to prove a motive. All the prosecutor has to do is prove that the perpetrator committed the crime, not why, although where a motive is established it may strengthen a case in the minds of the jurors.

Senior Constable Graham Richards was the first witness. He said that he initially interviewed Graham Stafford on Wednesday 25 September, and obtained a signed statement relating to his knowledge of Leanne's disappearance. Richards also took possession of the clothes Graham had worn on Monday – a pair of Broncos football shorts, a pair of joggers, a pair of black and red underpants and a blue work shirt – as well as the Gemini sedan.

Richards described the finding of the maggot in the car boot, which was 'on top of the rubber lining of the boot. This maggot was approximately fifteen millimetres in length and was of a dark colour. It was still alive and wriggling,' he testified. Photographs and videotape of the house, the car and the disposal site were tendered as evidence. Videotaped interviews with Graham were introduced into evidence and played to the court, and transcripts provided to the jurors. The remainder of the first day of the trial was taken up with the viewing of videos.

At the beginning of the second day, Graham's defence counsel Mr Clark drew the attention of the judge to an article in the morning edition of *The Courier-Mail*. The article reported part of Bullock's opening address and Clark felt it could influence the jury because it claimed that 'Blood found in Leanne's family home and in the boot of Stafford's car matched Leanne's extremely rare blood type. DNA testing on blood in Stafford's car excluded the blood belonging to 98.9 per cent of the population.' Mr Justice Derrington warned the jury against taking into account media articles relating to the trial, especially no doubt, the incorrect media report about the DNA results. For most of that day the court viewed the rest of the videotapes of the investigation and police interviews of Graham. Towards the end of the afternoon, Clark cross-examined Richards and the following exchange took place about finding the maggot:

> Mr Clark: Can you just show me your entry please, or the record you took of when you found the maggot?
> Richards: I was with Crick at the time when the maggot was found and Crick was to take possession of the maggot when it was found.
> Mr Clark: I appreciate what you are saying, but can you show me your entry, the record you took of when you saw the maggot?
> Richards: I took that entry into my memory.

Detective Fynes-Clinton came to the stand next and supported Richards' evidence. Despite strong objections from the Crown, the judge permitted Clark to raise the subject of Julie-Ann Lowe's murder at Goodna just three weeks after the death of Leanne.

A new witness, Detective Wardhaugh, gave brief evidence and confirmed he was responsible for recording and tagging all the exhibits located during the police investigation of Leanne Holland's murder. When asked: 'Do you know if a hammer was taken possession of?' Wardhaugh responded: 'I don't know, I couldn't say.' The issue of Graham's hammer, where it was and who had possession of it, was to become very significant.

The police had presumably taken it from the house and it was referred to in one of the taped video interviews. Yet, from reading the transcripts, the hammer seems to have simply vanished from the bedside table where it was last seen by Melissa and was never presented at the trial or in any subsequent court proceedings.

Leanne's father Terry was next and he confirmed that Leanne had telephoned him at work on the Monday morning and this resurrected the issue of her hair being dyed. Terry agreed he had two brief phone conversations, first with Leanne and then with Melissa, about the blonding of her hair.

Terry reiterated his surprise that Leanne was barefoot when she left the house on Monday morning, because she would wear shoes even to go the corner shop, a short distance away. He admitted it was his fault that a 'pornographic' videotape was found in Leanne's bedroom. He also agreed that it was usually his task to put out the wheelie bin onto the street for collection, but claimed that neither he nor Melissa had done it the day Leanne disappeared.

The implication was that Graham must have done it and yet no blood or other relevant evidence was found in the bin. On the third day of the trial, Terry was cross-examined on the proximity of the neighbouring houses, the hotel across the road and volume of the road traffic outside his front door, as well as about the cut to Leanne's foot.

Melissa took her father's place when he left the witness box. She was asked to describe the clothes Leanne wore to the party on the Friday night before her death. She confirmed that none of Leanne's shoes were missing and that Terry usually put out the rubbish bin. She also said she found nothing untoward at the house when she returned from work on Monday. Melissa told the court that Graham used to keep a fold-up chair in his car boot to use when he watched her netball games. The week that Leanne went missing, Melissa found the chair in the spare bedroom. When she asked Graham about it, he replied that he had cleaned the car and taken the chair out because it was rattling around. The prosecutor contended that he did so in order to fit Leanne's body in the boot. Then the final family member, Leanne's brother Craig, told the jury and the packed court that he had cut his hand in a drunken brawl and had bled in the house.

The next witness was Katrina Castle, a sixteen year old who went to school with Leanne. She said she saw Leanne at St Ives Shopping Centre around 7.30 a.m. on Monday 23 September.

Katrina said she could pinpoint the time because her father had made a withdrawal from an automatic teller machine. The time and date were on the receipt. She saw Leanne wearing a T-shirt, a dark-coloured jumper, perhaps purple or black, and black bicycle pants down to about her knees. She was wearing no shoes and carried a blue shopping bag.

The parade of eyewitnesses continued with 24-year-old bottle shop attendant Shane Cushway testifying that he saw Leanne outside her home at about 8.30 a.m. on that Monday morning. Cushway said he knew Leanne and easily recognised her.

Jason Farrell, aged 14, who knew Leanne from school, told the court he saw her in her front yard between 7.50 a.m. and 8 a.m. He described her as wearing black air pants and a black T-shirt. Farrell said Leanne told him she was going to go to the shops and that she intended peroxiding her hair.

A major prosecution witness was a forensic entomologist employed by the CSIRO in Adelaide, Beryl Morris. She held a degree in science and an honours degree in entomology and was enrolled in a Master's degree in agricultural science. She had given evidence or conducted investigations in more than 100 cases in various Australian states since 1977.

In this case she began by defining her discipline as 'the study of insects, and that is of use because some insects like to breed in decomposing material'. Ms Morris described three vials (numbered 1, 2 and 3 with a felt pen) containing maggots that she had received from the police for examination. There were two maggots in the first, about fifteen or more in the second and only a single maggot in the vial labelled 3. Her recollection of the single maggot in vial 3 differed from that of Senior Constable Bennett.

Ms Morris described this specimen as being larger than the other maggots and having food in its crop; whereas Bennett had described it as being shrivelled and desiccated. Ms Morris also said that the maggots were known as *Calliphora stygia* not *Lucilia cuprina* as they had been identified by Bennett.

Using temperature data supplied by the police, she estimated Leanne could not have died later than 5.30 a.m. on Tuesday 24 September. Ms Morris claimed it was more likely the eggs had been laid the previous day and conceded that 'the fly development times I think are ... an estimate of minimum time elapsed, but they're certainly not definitive'.

Other material witnesses were then called to give evidence. Fourteen-year-old schoolgirl Belinda Collins told the court she saw Leanne in Queen Street walking towards the Cecil Hotel at around 10 a.m. on Monday, dressed in a purple jumper and a black skirt.

Aged pensioner Michael Radcliffe of Queen Street said he saw a young man working on a car in Terry's yard, between 11 a.m. and noon, although he was not certain which day. Graham's former housemate Arthur Power confirmed that Stafford was at his house for half to three-quarters of an hour on the Monday. During his visit, Graham had acted 'perfectly normal'. He also told the court that he was normally an early riser, but had slept in that morning.

Factory hand and first-aid officer Cynthia Luckman, gave evidence that she inspected Graham's arm on the Tuesday morning at their work place. She described his injury as 'just a bit of swelling on the fleshy part here near the elbow'. Ms Luckman said that if Graham had not pointed the injury out to her, she would not have noticed it.

Police Transport Section mechanic Sergeant Kerry Carlton said he inspected Graham's Gemini sedan and saw a new shock absorber had been fitted, but that he observed no scratches to indicate that it had slipped off a jack.

On the trial's fourth day, the jury and court officials visited Leanne's Alice Street home and the bush off Redbank Plains Road where her body was found. When the trial reconvened in the courtroom, another crown witness, Michael Spinaze, recounted how he saw a hatchback or a station wagon, in that area of bush, one day during the week of Leanne's murder. It was between 6.20 and 6.30 a.m. when he was driving past on his way to work.

Aged pensioner Herbert Holland told the court that he was a great-uncle to Leanne. He recounted that he withdrew $200 from his account at the Goodna branch of the Commonwealth Bank on the Monday. He claimed that a male teller served him and he had not seen Leanne that day nor had she withdrawn money on his behalf.

The prosecution then called a forensic scientist from Adelaide, South Australia, Dr Angela van Daal, to attest to the DNA comparison, which matched blood samples taken from the bag and blanket with that of Leanne. The line-up of forensic experts continued with the pathologist Dr Ashby, who refused to accept that Leanne's hair colouring was due to blood staining and insisted her hair had been dyed. Ashby testified that Leanne had a blood alcohol content reading of .048 per cent and she also told the court the murder weapon was consistent with the type of hammer owned by Graham. That day a police fingerprint expert, Anthony Carstensen, gave evidence that he found no fingerprints on a green plastic garbage bag found beneath Leanne's body.

When Bill Crick came to the witness stand, he described his examination of the home and car. He said he believed the floors had been recently washed and told the court of the various swabs he took for later scientific testing. Crick described finding the maggot in Graham's car boot and said his find was witnessed by Detective Richards. He confirmed this significant piece of evidence had been neither recorded anywhere nor photographed. Crick told the court that he attended the scene where the body was found to carry out his own investigations. He described how he took maggots from the body and placed them in two vials for later scientific analysis. Crick also introduced into evidence overlays he had made of Graham's tyres to compare them with his photographs of the impressions. As a result of his comparison, Crick concluded the impressions matched the tyres on Graham's car.

Nineteen-year-old tyre fitter Tony Bashforth said in evidence on the fifth day of the trial that he had fitted tyres to Graham's car prior to the murder. Bashforth told the court no other tyre manufacturer made treads with patterns similar to the two different tread patterns found on Graham's car, the Bridgestone RD229 and SF340 tread patterns. Significant issues of similarities in tyre patterns and manufacturers were ignored when the state manager for Bridgestone Australia, Rodney Thomas, was called to give evidence. He was only asked to estimate the number of tyres of the RD229 pattern and the SF340 pattern sold in south-east Queensland.

The day ended with Queensland Government biochemist Kristine Bentley explaining the results of her analysis of the blood samples delivered to her by Crick. Bentley said she found blood on the blanket, Chux cloth and bag – taken from the boot of Graham's car – identical to Leanne's blood group.

Mr Thomas of Bridgestone Australia was recalled at the start of the sixth day of the trial and questioned about tyre sizes.

As Bullock wrapped up the prosecution case against Graham, he recalled Terry Holland and asked Leanne's height at the time she went missing. Melissa was also recalled briefly to clarify whether, at any point during the week of Leanne's murder, she opened the boot of Graham's car. She told the court she had not, but, in response to cross-examination by Mr Clark, agreed that she could have gone to the boot at any time and opened it with her own key.

In a criminal trial, an accused person is not obliged to give evidence or present their own witnesses on the basis that it is the prosecution's role to prove guilt. Graham Stafford elected to present evidence in his defence. In Queensland, by calling evidence the defence forfeits the right to make their final address to the jury last. Consequently this right is, by default, passed to the prosecution.

The defence called seven witnesses, beginning with Graham Stafford. The remainder were largely to give evidence about sightings of Leanne; and Constable Bennett to discuss the maggot evidence.

Crown Prosecutor Bullock cross-examined Graham at length. Graham consistently and emphatically denied that he had tortured or murdered Leanne and denied placing her body in the boot of his car and dumping it in the bush off Redbank Plains Road on the morning of Wednesday 25 September.

A defence witness was called who directly contradicted the evidence of prosecution witness Herbert Holland about his bank withdrawal on the Monday. Bank teller Audrey Tymon worked at the Goodna branch of the Commonwealth Bank.

She told the court that she had served a young female customer fitting the description of Leanne at about 11 a.m. on that Monday. Ms Tymon recalled the girl was wearing a long-sleeved black jacket or jumper with purple through it and a light coloured T-shirt. She could not see what the girl was wearing below counter height.

The owner of the Goodna Food Store, situated next to the Cecil Hotel in Queen Street, Kylie Stark, claimed Leanne entered her shop on the Monday afternoon. Ms Stark described Leanne as wearing dark pants or a skirt, a white shirt with a collar and a black vest. She said Leanne looked well dressed, as if she were going out somewhere. She agreed, however, with a suggestion from the prosecution that it might have been the previous Friday that she had seen Leanne.

When first interviewed by police on the Wednesday following Leanne's disappearance, however, when this memory was, no doubt, more fresh in her mind, she was adamant that Leanne had been in her shop twice on that Monday – the first time was around 3.05 p.m., when Ms Stark arrived at work to take over from her husband and the second between 3.30 p.m. and 3.40 p.m.

Another witness who claimed to have seen a young girl fitting Leanne's description on the Monday was Marjorie Rodgers, who gave the time as between 11 a.m. and midday. During that time, Ms Rodgers said she saw Leanne outside the Commonwealth Bank, Goodna branch, in the company of two young men.

The prosecutor challenged this sighting and claimed Rodgers was mistaken. Some years later, when Crowley was reviewing the police job logs, he noted that Marjorie Rodgers said she was with her son, who had gone to school with Leanne, and he was the one who had recognised her. It is not known whether the sighting was ever confirmed with the son. It is, however, known that no statement was taken from him and he did not give evidence at the trial, either for the prosecution or the defence.

Fourteen-year-old student Robert Baker told the court he had known Leanne for two years and had dated her. He recalled seeing Leanne as she was entering the Cecil Hotel across the road from her house about at 8.30 p.m. on Monday. Baker said he was about ten feet away from her and saw that she was wearing black tracksuit pants and a black jumper.

Under cross-examination, he admitted that it could have been the Sunday night when he saw her, but he was reasonably certain it was the Monday. The final witness for the day was Steven Marwick, who said he saw Leanne between 3.00 and 4 p.m. on Monday outside the Cecil Hotel.

The entire seventh day of the trial was taken up by the final addresses of the prosecution and defence, and on the eighth day, Mr Justice Derrington delivered his charge to the jury.

The judge went through every piece of evidence, telling the jury not to consider each matter separately, but to look at the combination of all of them. Several times he apologised for the length of his address, but assured the jury it was necessary to fully cover both the prosecution and defence evidence.

The judge completed his final charge at 2.45 that afternoon, when the jury retired to consider its verdict.

A little more than three hours later, at 5.57 p.m., the jury filed back into the jury box. They found Graham guilty of murdering Leanne and Mr Justice Derrington sentenced Graham to life imprisonment, saying:

Mr Stafford, you have been convicted of one of the most heinous crimes in the criminal calendar. There is only one possible sentence, and I sentence you to imprisonment for life. I do not make any recommendation that you never be released. However, I must say this – the punishment which you will now suffer is one which must horrify you, because indeed it is a horrifying future for you. I only hope that it will be a deterrent to others against crimes of violence, and particularly serious violence. There is too much violence in the community already, and people can be protected only by the sentences imposed by the court. I warn people disposed to violence that your terrible fate will fall upon them also if they offend in this way.

16

A family fights back

The Stafford family could simply not accept that their son had murdered Leanne – perhaps almost any family in this situation would feel the same. Despite being told by almost everyone that the evidence was overwhelming, they were not prepared to give up. They sought legal advice, and were told that there were some legal technicalities that might warrant grounds for a retrial. Accordingly, they funded Graham's appeal to the Queensland Court of Criminal Appeal.

Five months after his conviction his appeal was rejected and his original sentence reaffirmed. The family sought further legal advice and again were informed that there might be some slim legal grounds on which to appeal the conviction. The next and final step in the judicial process was an Application for Leave to Appeal to the High Court of Australia. In the meantime, the family decided to take action rather than sitting on their hands and awaiting the result of the application.

Eric and Jean Stafford made an appointment to see Graeme Crowley, a former police officer then working as a private investigator. When they entered his office in December 1992, they had an inexhaustible supply of hope and determination, but few real expectations of success. They told Crowley that they believed the evidence was open to serious question and that their son Graham had not committed this murder. Eric and Jean told him the horrifying story of their lives being turned upside down as first they learned of Leanne's disappearance, and then that their son was a murder suspect. During the trial, they told Crowley, their shock and disbelief evolved into anger as it became apparent to them that Graham did not and could not have committed this crime.

Crowley suggested to Eric and Jean that the best place to begin would be with the police evidence. It would be a case of rechecking all the evidence the police had gathered to test it for accuracy. It was also essential to verify the police had not overlooked anything vital to the case. Eric and Jean wanted other steps taken too, but agreed to start with the evidence. Crowley explained to Jean and Eric that such inquiries are often double-edged, in that evidence exonerating the convicted person might be found, but it was also possible that evidence that further implicated the accused could also be unearthed. Jean responded that, if there was evidence implicating Graham in the murder, they would just have to accept it and get on with their lives.

To Crowley, an experienced investigator, it did seem at first that the Crown had a strong forensic and circumstantial case. There were, however, essential differences from other cases, i.e. no eyewitnesses and no apparent motive. The test would be whether or not the evidence would survive the intense scrutiny he planned to place upon it, because, except for those issues challenged by the defence counsel during the trial, such as the later sightings of Leanne, the evidence had been largely uncontested.

Crowley knew it was not necessary to prove motive in a criminal trial, but his experience had taught him that the key to solving any case was indeed motive. Graham had no history of antisocial behaviour, no underlying mental problems likely to cause him to go off the rails so suddenly and viciously, and there was no evidence that he had ever acted in any suspect or offensive way towards Leanne, either physically or verbally.

It was very clear from the early evidence that the police originally thought Graham had helped Leanne to dye her hair in the bathroom of the house they shared and then appeared to lie about it. Police hinted at a scenario in which Leanne was partially dressed and was alone with Graham. It was some weeks before it was established that Leanne's hair had not been dyed, which weakened this theory, but by then it was too late. Events were in motion. Graham had already been arrested and the myth of Leanne's dyed hair would endure.

Crowley was intrigued by timing – minimal time had been available to Graham Stafford to murder Leanne. He would have had to have killed her before lunch on that Monday to allow him sufficient time to clean up the bloody mess, hide the body and compose himself before Terry and Melissa arrived home. He noted the considerable number of sightings of Graham during the period in question. He wondered when he could possibly have had time to commit the murder. His best estimate was that Graham needed a minimum of two hours to molest and torture Leanne, kill her, further molest her corpse, hide it and then clean up. Crowley studied all the available material, but simply could not find two consecutive hours in which Graham could have done all this.

Before Crowley had a chance to finish his inquiries, Stafford's legal process reached the next and final stage. On 5 March 1993 the High Court handed down its rejection of Graham's Application for Leave to Appeal. Once the High Court rejected his application all avenues of legal redress were exhausted. Nevertheless, Eric and Jean asked Crowley to continue with his review of all the material. They were not sure where this would lead, but refused to give up on their son. With the High Court appeal rejected, Crowley believed Stafford had no further avenues open to him. He had heard of a Petition to the Governor, but had no personal knowledge of how the process worked. Crowley continued with his review of the evidence as requested, but the usual pressure of a court appointed deadline had been removed.

As he delved deeper into the case, however, and identified a growing list of problems with the evidence, his doubts increased. When he realised how focused the detectives had been on Graham as the primary suspect from the very beginning, his concerns increased further. Crowley wondered if any of the investigators ever considered that Graham might not have had the opportunity or the motive to kill Leanne or that the evidence did not really fit the crime.

Crowley started looking at those witnesses who supported the circumstantial evidence. He was intrigued by the supposed sightings of Graham's car in the bush enclave where Leanne's body was found. Michael Spinaze and another witness, Lynette Mende, were the only two witnesses the police had produced, but they were not the only witnesses to approach police about sightings of cars near where Leanne's body was discovered. Crowley observed that there was even a note in Crick's handwritten record that when he returned to the crime scene the day after Leanne's body was found, he observed a Ford Falcon station wagon parked at the bottom of the bush track.

There was, however, nothing to show that any check was made of that vehicle or its occupant and it was not mentioned in evidence at the trial.

Michael Spinaze claimed to have seen a car similar to Graham's on the bush track where the body was found. He could not remember the exact day he saw the car on the track and his uncertainty is reflected in the statement he made to detectives on Saturday 28 September:

I recall that on either Tuesday the 24th or Wednesday the 25th of September, 1991, I was being driven to work by a friend, Craig Ferguson. He picks me up outside the Redbank Plains Tavern at about 6.15 a.m., and we drive to work along Redbank Plains Road. We go this way all the time. I recall that when we went past the intersection of Greenwood Village Road I saw a small red coloured car reversing out on a dirt track which leads to beehives. I don't recall what type of car it was, only that it was a small type car like a Laser or a Charade, that size; it was a hatch or wagon, but not a sedan. The car was about 30 metres up the track, and there was only the driver. The time would have been between 6.20 a.m. and 6.30 a.m. The car seemed to be in good condition and appeared to be maintained and polished because it was shiny. There didn't seem to be any rust on it.

When Crowley spoke with Spinaze some years after Graham's trial, he was unable to expand on his original evidence other than being 'certain the car was a hatch or a station wagon and not a sedan'. It is clear that Spinaze could not stipulate the day of the week nor the type of car that he sighted.

Thirty-three year old mother of three Lynette Mende was driving along Redbank Plains Road, towards Ipswich, on the Wednesday morning that the prosecution alleged Graham dumped Leanne's body – which he had supposedly been hiding in his car boot since Monday. She was headed west and in a line of traffic near the intersection of Greenwood Village Road. A van in front of her braked suddenly and she was forced to brake hard to avoid an accident. Her statement to police a week later recorded the following:

> This van had to stop for another white car, which turned off suddenly over the double white lines and started to enter the tracks off to my right. These are the tracks which are right near the sign which says Redbank Plains. As I slowed down I noticed a vehicle which was parked on the top track in front of the rocky outcrop. I saw that the boot of the vehicle was open. I couldn't see anyone around when I looked, as I thought it was strange that a vehicle would be parked there. I recall that the vehicle was a sedan and that it was a reddy brown colour and I think that the headlights were a square shape. I think the vehicle was either a Gemini or a Sunbird. It wasn't the early Gemini, it would have been around a 1980 model.

At Graham's trial, Mr Justice Derrington cautioned the jury against accepting the evidence given by Lynette Mende. The judge was not suggesting that Mende was lying or in any sense unreliable; he was simply concerned that police had shown her a photograph of Graham's car immediately before the Supreme Court trial six months after the events in question, and that her recollection might have been influenced by it.

He went to the extraordinary length of directing the jury that they not use any of Mende's evidence to do with her description of Graham's car. Mende's evidence to the court had changed from sighting a 'reddy brown sedan with square headlights being possibly a Gemini or Sunbird' to 'a reddish brown sedan with square headlights, about the size of a Gemini, an aerial on the roof, an O'Neill sticker across the top of the windscreen, and sporting a sunroof '.

Crowley felt the most unusual part of Mende's evidence related to the sightings of two vehicles that day. She claimed that there was one vehicle at the top of the track and another vehicle, a white van that she thought was driving up the track to meet it. In his view this presented a dilemma for the prosecution. If there was a second vehicle involved in the murder then, at the very least, Graham couldn't have acted alone. Crowley interviewed Lyn Mende in 1994 and asked her about the white van she had seen. She was keen to help and said:

> At the time I felt it [the white van] was connected with the other car that I saw up the track. I thought the white van was going up the track to meet the other car. I told police I thought it was connected. My children looked out the back window of my car and saw the van. They said it was like an old ambulance. My kids saw this white ambulance van about a month ago and recognised it, and said that was the one they had seen at the track … I have to say, when I saw the photograph of Graham Stafford's car I was a bit surprised by the colour. It was bright red, but the car I saw was darker in colour, but I put that down to the shade from the rocky outcrop on the car up the track.

The original job log of her contact with police records this: 'Lynette Mende recalls seeing a brown coloured old car near the area of the scene at about 8 a.m. on Tuesday morning'. Crowley was concerned that this changed to Wednesday morning with no apparent explanation. He was also concerned that the change in her evidence from a brown coloured car to the sighting of Graham's Gemini with its boot lid up at the top of that track was allowed to go unchallenged.

Crowley reviewed some of the other sightings recorded in the

Crime Investigation Log that was handed to Graham's lawyer in 1997 only after repeated requests. At 11 a.m. on the Monday Leanne went missing, a green Holden sedan with four or five occupants was seen in the vicinity of the disposal site. The registered owner of the vehicle was interviewed and denied being there, but there is no mention of whether the occupants were found and questioned. On the same day, at about 2.30 p.m., a man told police he had see a silver hatchback and a blue Nissan Pulsar close to where Leanne's body had been dumped.

When he approached, he found a middle-aged couple having sexual intercourse in one of the cars. Police were also told that on Tuesday 24 September at about 11.30 a.m., a dark blue Commodore sedan was seen on the same bush track. An Aboriginal male, aged about seventeen to twenty, was seen nearby, carrying what appeared to be a bundle of clothing. Once again, the police log did not record any inquiries being made to determine the identity of this person.

Another report made to the police was, that at about 6.30 a.m. on Wednesday, two light-coloured Japanese-type sedans were seen near the beehives on the bush track and two males were seen nearby.

Two witnesses independently told police that at about 6.30 a.m. on the next day, a green Ford Falcon sedan was seen emerging from the bush track near the beehives.

The police logs did not record what inquiries if any were made to locate these various vehicles and their occupants.

Regrettably, no evidence of any of these sightings near the disposal scene was ever put before the jury. These sightings were obviously contrary to the evidence against Graham Stafford. In addition, the owner of the adjacent land had previously informed police that there were always cars up there. When Crowley called on her during his investigation, the owner reiterated that plenty of cars frequented the supposedly isolated site.

In 1993 and 1994 the media started to take an interest in the case. Two short television stories were produced on the subject. Brisbane reporter for *The Sunday Mail*, Darrell Giles, took a particular interest in the story. Giles started writing articles on the family's insistence on the court getting it wrong. This resulted in a number of potential witnesses contacting Crowley and Wilson with information, not always conclusive. As the discrepancies mounted and the family's suspicions were confirmed, they decided they would seek further legal advice on presenting a Petition to the Governor while awaiting the final outcome of Crowley's inquiries.

In the meantime, Crowley found that other sightings had not been reported to police. Another resident of Redbank, Doris Kudelka, a neighbour of Lynette Mende, also saw the reddish-brown car up the bush track that week. She knew Mende had told police what she saw. Kudelka did not therefore think it necessary for her to become involved at that stage.

It was two years after Leanne's murder, in 1993, when she saw a photograph of Graham Stafford's car in a television program that Ms Kudelka realised the reddish-brown car she saw on the bush track that day was definitely not Graham's car.

Her recollection of the car she saw was of an old Gemini hatchback, brownish in colour or undercoated brown. Kudelka was positive the car she saw was not a gleaming red Gemini or anything like it. Crowley took Ms Kudelka to the site and she confirmed that she saw the car in the same bushland area as the one seen by Mende. Later, in a shopping centre car park, Kudelka showed Crowley a car that in her opinion was similar to the one she had seen on the bush track that morning. Crowley noted that the car did not resemble Stafford's in colour or shape.

Another woman came forward in 1994 and told Crowley she had also seen cars in the bush the week of Leanne's murder. She described a large white panel van, like an old ambulance; and a smaller, brownish car. She believed the smaller car to be an older model Cortina. This woman had previously owned a Gemini and believed the car she had seen was not the same. She saw two men at the open boot of the old brown car. She claimed to have gone to the police later, but they appeared not to be interested in what she had seen. These extra sightings contradicted the evidence of Spinaze and Mende, which had not been definitive. The colour was wrong, so was the make and body shape, and neither of them was even sure of the day.

17

Reinvestigation

Continuing with his investigations, Crowley determined that he needed to interview as many people as possible who had seen Leanne prior to her disappearance. Many of the young people who might have had information, even from the time of the end-of-term party, were not interviewed by police in those early days. In 1993, Crowley tried to talk with some of these young people, but their parents refused access. These parents, not unreasonably, thought the process would be too upsetting for their children; Crowley let it go.

He was nevertheless determined to talk to Leanne's closest friend, Trisha Lynch. She was difficult to trace, but Crowley eventually located her in 1993, living on the streets of Sydney's notorious Kings Cross. He tracked her to a homeless teenagers' refuge and immediately flew to Sydney to interview her in the presence of a hostel supervisor.

She appeared to be suffering the after-effects of some type of intoxicating drug and looked much older than her sixteen years. She was aggressive, uninterested and somewhat uncooperative. When asked if she had any evidence other than that already known by police, she volunteered that Graham had looked at her 'in a funny way' one day when she was at Leanne's house. By contrast, she also said that she had been in the house several times alone with Graham, or with him and Leanne, and he had never touched her or made any inappropriate suggestions to either of them. She went further, admitting that Leanne had never complained to her about any untoward comments or advances by Graham. She also told Crowley that she had introduced Sean McPhedran to Leanne and that they had all played together on a number of occasions.

Close friends of Graham Stafford's were also contacted for further information. Bob Neyndorff told Crowley he had never seen a dark side to Graham and always thought of him as a gentle person, incapable of committing the crime for which he had been convicted. Prior to his arrest for Leanne's murder, Graham had never run foul of the law in any way. He had never been arrested for any offence nor even received a traffic ticket. He was aged 28 when arrested and, although a motor mechanic by trade, had been employed by his then employer as a process worker for over four years.

Crowley spent considerable time retracing the steps of the police and seeking out those people who claimed to have seen Leanne, even when the police had not followed up on them.

He spoke to the woman who saw Leanne with an Aboriginal female. He tracked down the man who said he was in the Cecil Hotel and saw Leanne at around 3.30 p.m. on the Monday. It was some years since he made his statement, but the man revealed that he was under considerable pressure from family and friends at the time to change his statement and concede that he was mistaken about which day he saw Leanne outside the pub.

When he spoke to Crowley, however, he was still convinced it was Leanne and it was at the time and on the day he originally stated.

It was the police case that Graham murdered Leanne in her home sometime after 8 a.m. but before 4.40 p.m. on Monday 23 September. He then secreted her body in the boot of his car, dumping it in the bush early the following Wednesday morning, when Melissa recognised his car driving from the wrong direction on his way to work.

The prosecutor alleged that Graham murdered Leanne by bashing her around the head a number of times with a heavy blunt object, possibly a hammer. In the course of this attack he caused blood to be left in the house and in the boot of his car. He also alleged that

Graham injured himself during his attack on Leanne. Mr Bullock acknowledged that after 4.40 p.m. Graham had an alibi; Melissa arrived home around that time and Graham was in her company throughout Monday night. On Tuesday morning he went to work and stayed there all day. Together Graham, Melissa and Terry reported Leanne missing on the Tuesday night. Throughout Wednesday, after his aborted trip to work and to Arthur Power's place, he and Melissa were in the company of investigating police. The Crown went so far as to say that if Leanne was not murdered before 4.40 p.m. on that Monday, then Graham was not the murderer. The prosecution was confident it had the right man for the crime.

Crowley was especially disturbed by police references to Leanne's disappearance as a murder case before her body was discovered. Documents showed that detectives rostered for duty at Goodna Police Station on that Wednesday were not considered experienced enough to handle the investigation.

Police witnesses later insisted it was nothing more than a missing person inquiry. Yet the same documents suggested they took the disappearance very seriously from the outset. There were a number of individual references to Graham and the job logs suggested anything, but a missing person investigation with no suspect.

When reviewing the investigation, Crowley wondered why there was an instruction to police that they ascertain what Graham was wearing at the time of his visit to the police station, his means of transport as well as any observations about his demeanour or state of mind.

In his experience, police must have had some information to compel them to focus on Graham's clothing, transportation and especially his state of mind and alibi at such an early point in their enquiries.

The investigation into Leanne's disappearance had at that time been in progress for about four hours. The early hours and days of such a case are usually taken up with gathering all the known information concerning the missing person and his or her last known movements, together with establishing all those persons who had contact with her. This information is normally then analysed before further action is considered. It seemed as if the investigators must have been privy to some confidential information about Graham, Leanne or both.

Particular entries in the job log relating to Graham were intriguing. In one instance some investigators were detailed to visit the Goodna Medical Centre. They were to obtain particulars of the nature of Graham's supposed arm injury – the time he attended the surgery and what clothing he was wearing during his visits.

They were also instructed to inquire as to his state of mind. Similarly, detectives were to visit neighbours to find anyone who may have seen Graham working on his car in the yard. They were to find out if anyone had seen Leanne leave in his car and if anyone witnessed him injuring himself.

These were not the only instances where Graham seemed to be targeted that first day of investigation. Another job log referred to a Redbank Plains resident who had heard a girl screaming in a passing car. He described the car as a bright red sedan, possibly a Ford Cortina. Crowley would not have taken any notice of the police report except the officer who filed it made the comment that the witness did not think the car could be a Gemini. No effort was apparently made to locate this vehicle or its occupants.

The next piece of evidence to be reconsidered was the mop and bucket allegedly used to clean up the crime scene. It does seem incredible that Graham could have cleaned these items so completely that no blood could be detected. It is doubtful that Graham would have half filled the bucket with dirty water, after completely disposing of all scientific evidence, so that no one would become suspicious. For one thing, there was so little time – not only to do such a thorough clean up of the house, but then to remove any traces of evidence from the cleaning utensils.

Whether viewed as a crime of anger or one of care and calculation, it seems extremely unlikely that Graham was either that devious or forensically sophisticated. Police inquiries at the convenience shop around the corner revealed Graham bought no cleaning goods there that day. For the prosecution case to be credible he must have gone further afield, but this would have limited further the time he had on that day to do everything of which the prosecution accused him.

Many months later, in trawling through the large assortment of documents and other exhibits that all murder cases accumulate, Crowley noted the contents of a receipt from the government forensic laboratory dated and timed 11.35 a.m., Thursday 26 September, which indicated Senior Constable Crick had delivered various items for forensic examination.

It would be highly irregular for exhibits to be delivered to the forensic laboratory and a receipt issued at a later time or day, because the continuity of possession of exhibits is crucial to proving a case. The receipt was titled: 'Re: Murder of Holland', yet at that time, on that date, there was supposedly no direct evidence the case was a homicide. Certainly, the body had not been found and at the trial Crick told the court that at that time it was only a missing person investigation.

Crick stated at the trial that he had commenced his examination of Stafford's car at police headquarters at 11 a.m. on that Thursday morning. The same documents disclosed that Crick had found, again, the maggot in the boot, an hour later at midday. As the forensic laboratory is at the other end of town to police headquarters, it is not clear how Crick could be in both places at once. If he suspended his examination of Graham's car to travel to the laboratory and transfer exhibits, his notes and later evidence did not reflect this.

Police photographs since handed to the defence team show what appeared to be three unlit cigarettes in close proximity to the body, but records indicate that police did not take possession of them nor consider them significant. Police throughout Australia and around the world follow similar procedures at major crime scenes. All evidence, regardless of its size or significance is collected and recorded.

In most cases, a crime scene is actually vacuumed to ensure that every single particle of evidence is collected. Such evidence may not become relevant for days, months or years.

To discard evidence at the scene is contrary to best police investigation techniques. To fail to produce it later is contrary to the rules of natural justice. As Graham did not smoke, and as there are allegations that burn marks were on Leanne's body, this could have been highly significant evidence.

While recognising the time constraints under which Dr Ashby examined Leanne's body at the site where it was found, and later in conducting the autopsy, it is reasonable to assert that the examination may not have been sufficiently thorough for a murder investigation and could have gone much further. For example, particles of brain matter, blood and hair could have been found on the murder weapon, or evidence from the murder weapon could have been shown to exist on the body. In particular, indentations in the skull fractures would 'fit' the shape of the instrument used. A review of the evidence indicates that there was apparently no comparison made between the skull fractures and the hammer police took from Graham.

Furthermore, Ashby should have been able to give evidence on whether the killer was left or right-handed and whether Leanne had been standing, crouching, sitting or lying down at the time the injuries were inflicted. It would have been useful to know if the blows were inflicted from the front, back or side of the victim. This type of evidence can be crucial in piecing together the crime and identifying the offender.

The lack of depth in the forensic examination is also demonstrated with regard to Leanne's specific injuries. It was never stated whether samples were taken of the foreign matter in the knife wound next to Leanne's anus and if so whether the material was checked against samples taken from the place where her body was found. Dirt and grass samples taken from Leanne's house would have been useful for comparison purposes.

The rules of evidence state that evidence found must be presented. The rules of natural justice require that evidence that exonerates or even weakens the case against the accused also be presented. Some legal counsel would argue that this point alone would be sufficient grounds to apply for an order to exhume Leanne's body for further scientific tests.

Dr Ashby's terminology additionally implies that the injuries were inflicted after death in some kind of sadomasochistic ritual. Yet, if these were post-mortem injuries, the killer would have denied himself the very gratification he apparently sought.

At the trial, the Crown willingly accepted the pathologist's interpretation. In addition, there was apparently no testing done on stomach contents to eliminate the consumption of alcohol. If Leanne had consumed alcohol, when and where it happened was a crucial part of reconstructing her last movements.

18

The maggot tale

The first significant error Crowley found in the police case concerned Leanne's time of death. The Crown did not dispute that Leanne was murdered after 8 a.m. but before 4.30 p.m. on Monday 23 September. Outside those hours, Graham had an alibi that had been checked and crosschecked by police.

The forensic entomologist Beryl Morris held the key to establishing precisely when Leanne died. She gave convincing evidence at trial that it was before 5.30 a.m. on Tuesday, with the most probable time of death being between 4.00 and 6.00 p.m. the previous day. This evidence alone disturbed Crowley, as it was on the very periphery of the available time for Stafford to have committed the crime. However, he appeared to be alone in this concern.

Morris calculated the growth rate of the maggots on air temperatures supplied by Bill Crick for the Ipswich area for the relevant days. Inquiries made to the Australian Bureau of Meteorology showed that there were in fact several data recording stations in the Brisbane area. The western section of the city was covered by weather stations at Archerfield and further west at Ipswich. Crowley noted that the temperatures Crick supplied to Morris were actually recorded at Archerfield, about eighteen kilometres from where Leanne's body was found. The weather station at Ipswich was only seven kilometres away from the scene and the temperatures recorded there were on average two degrees higher than those at Archerfield. The temperatures as supplied by Crick and recorded at Archerfield and those from Ipswich in September 1991 were:

| | Archerfield | | Ipswich | |
	maximum	minimum	maximum	minimum
Monday 23	25° C	8° C	27° C	10° C
Tuesday 24	28° C	14° C	31° C	15° C
Wednesday 25	25° C	18° C	27° C	18° C
Thursday 26	30° C	13° C	31° C	14° C

Key to Crowley's investigation was to find out what difference, if any, higher temperatures would have on the growth rate of the maggots. He contacted Beryl Morris by letter, supplying her with the new data from the Ipswich office of the meteorological department and asked her to recalculate the estimated time of death. He then waited for her response as weeks passed with agonising slowness.

When it came, Morris told him that the most probable time of Leanne's death, based on the more accurate data, was around 10 a.m. on Tuesday 24 September. Despite personal scepticism about being able to pinpoint the exact time of death by calculating the growth rate of maggots, Crowley was excited by this significant development in the case.

Morris was unquestionably the most qualified and experienced forensic entomologist in Australia. In addition, her estimate was based on the assumption that Leanne's body was exposed to the elements from the time she died to the time her body was found. Her calculations did not take into consideration the time Leanne's body was supposedly in the boot of Graham's car, which would have been considerably hotter than the temperature outside. Therefore, the time of death could be even later on Tuesday.

Crowley decided to try an experiment. Weeks passed as he watched the weather, checking the temperature daily until the local weather patterns were similar to those in September 1991. The Stafford family was on standby to make Graham's car available quickly and in October 1993, conditions were about as close as they would get to what Crowley needed.

He hired a thermo hygrograph, which continuously records temperature and humidity on a graph paper printout. He placed the machine in the boot of Graham's car and parked it in Redbank Plains for four days. When he checked the machine's readings he found the temperature in the car boot reached 44° Celsius when the outside temperature was 31°. When the outside minimum temperature dropped to 14°, the boot temperature was just 11°.

He again wrote to Beryl Morris asking her to recalculate the time of death using these new data. Crowley worried that the entomologist might have become weary of his repeated pleas for help, but Morris came through and sent him another statement indicating Leanne's time of death was in the afternoon of Tuesday 24 September.

In the meantime, Graham Stafford's parents instructed solicitor Richard Carew to explore the possibility of preparing a Petition to the Governor – the only avenue of appeal left open. Carew was meticulous about preparing this new evidence in such a way that it could not be easily challenged.

To cover the possibilities, Carew asked Morris to calculate the time of death using five different scenarios:

- The body was dumped, uncovered, in bushland on the morning of Wednesday 25 September 1991;
- The body was dumped around the same time, but wrapped in some insulating material;
- The body was insulated and contained in a car boot before being dumped on the Wednesday morning;
- It was in the car boot, but not wrapped in insulating material before being dumped at about 8 a.m. on the Wednesday.
- A straight comparison using the original temperatures as supplied by Crick with the temperatures obtained by Crowley.

The final calculations from Beryl Morris for the various scenarios set the time of Leanne's death as between 10 a.m. and 6.30 p.m. on Tuesday. With the new data, Morris had now rejected the time of death as having occurred on the Monday. On her new and more accurate findings, Graham could not have committed the murder.

Morris is the first to admit that forensic entomology is not capable of complete accuracy and describes her estimate of time of death as a 'best guess'.

The prosecution, however, was always well aware of the limitations of her science, but was still happy to call her as an expert witness, especially as she was and remains the leading Australian expert on forensic entomology. The fact that she put the day of Leanne's death as the Tuesday rather than the Monday was more significant than the actual hour of death.

When Crowley finally met Beryl Morris face to face in Sydney in 1993, she said she would much prefer to simply give police a day of death rather than a time of death. Indeed, concerning the original report she supplied to Detective Fynes-Clinton, Morris made the following comments in her affidavit to Richard Carew:

Due to the haste with which I prepared the report and lack of accurate information concerning matters such as the time of sunrise, the report was in the nature of a preliminary report and I am certain that I informed the Queensland Police of this fact. I recall, for example, informing Detective Fynes-Clinton that I had, for the purposes of the report, assumed that sunrise in the relevant area was similar to Adelaide, which in September is approximately 6.30 a.m. I must say that I am used to my first report in criminal cases being considered as a preliminary report. In my experience, a report such as this is normally followed by further information being forwarded to me and/or conferences being held prior to my being called to give evidence.

No such consultation took place and based on Morris's first report, the prosecutor called her as a witness. Her new evidence, based on more accurate data, apart from any other discrepancies in the police case, should be sufficient for this case to be reinvestigated.

If Leanne did not die on the Monday, then the Crown case fails. The Court of Appeal, to which the Govenor's Petition was referred, unfortunately and conveniently disposed of Morris's revised findings by pointing to the ambiguity inherent in entomological evidence. Basically, the court decided Morris did not know when Leanne died.

There is also now a question mark over the numbering of the vials containing the maggots taken from the body and from the car. Crick told the court that after finding the lone maggot at about midday on Thursday, he placed it in a vial and numbered it. Crowley wondered what number he gave it.

Unfortunately, Crick was never asked. Constable Bennett, the first entomologist, said there was a number 3 on the vial. Forensic entomologist Beryl Morris agreed, with the other two containing maggots taken from the body being numbered 1 and 2.

The evidence clearly showed the single maggot was taken from the car at noon. The maggots were taken from the body at around 5 p.m. the same day. At midday the body had not been found.

It is not clear then why the first vial would be given the number 3 and subsequent ones numbered 1 and 2.

Unfortunately, no one has been able to ascertain why the vials were numbered in reverse order and what the significance of this might be.

Years later, on 5 March 2006, reporter Darrell Giles broke yet another sensational story in *The Sunday Mail*. He reported that forensic scientist Russell Luke had been asked by the prosecution in 1997 to review the evidence in preparation for the forthcoming Petition appeal, but alleges that, because his report was unfavourable, it was ignored. Giles wrote:

He says his report would have discounted much of the prosecution evidence. 'I had serious questions about much of the evidence', Mr Luke said yesterday. 'My report would have said that much of the forensic evidence should have been totally ignored ... it should not have been part of the police case.' Mr Luke went on to raise doubts about the following issues:

Why was the lone maggot found in the boot longer and fatter than the maggots found on the body 36 hours later, and how did it manage to survive so long without food and moisture?

Why didn't police remove the live lone maggot in the boot when they claimed to have first found it, instead of 24 hours later?

Why was there no written, photographic or videotape record of the initial find?

Why did police not DNA-test the gut content of the maggot to confirm it had come from the body?

Why didn't the boot have more maggots, a smell, blood or other body fluids or other conclusive evidence the body had been there for two days?

'It would have been very hard, if not impossible, to get that dead smell out of the boot – out of anything', he said.

'They have used that maggot to try to prove that the body was in the boot. But the maggot evidence is tarnished ... it should have been ignored, thrown out.'

Mr Luke went onto say that maggots need food and moisture to survive and, once removed from their food source, quickly shrivel and die. 'Given the period of time that elapsed ... it just doesn't add up.'

19

The bank teller

There are, of course, many other serious problems with the police and prosecution case, not the least being the number of people who claimed to have seen Leanne not only on the day the police say she was killed but, in some cases, after the time she was alleged to have been killed.

For example, the mystery of whether Leanne was in the Goodna branch of the Commonwealth Bank on the Monday has never been satisfactorily resolved. The Crown case was that Herbert Holland, Leanne's great-uncle, withdrew money from his own account and that the bank teller, Audrey Tymon, was mistaken when she told the court she served a young girl fitting Leanne's description.

The evidence to support Tymon's claim has grown significantly since the trial. Crowley in fact found the majority of this evidence was available to the police at the time of the investigation, but was apparently ignored or overlooked.

Herbert Holland gave sworn evidence that he was served by a male teller yet there were no male tellers at that bank at that time. More importantly, the withdrawal slip used in the transaction has the initial 'a' written on it, which Tymon has identified as her signature. Other bank staff also verified to Crowley that this was her signature.

This is important for two reasons. First, it confirms that Tymon handled the transaction. Secondly, it confirms that the signature on the withdrawal slip had been verified against the specimen signature held at the bank. According to Tymon, this is normal practice only when a party not a signatory to an account withdraws money from that account. Tymon further claimed she particularly remembered the transaction because she took notice of a young girl withdrawing a large amount of cash out of a joint account holding a considerable balance.

Herbert Holland's passbook has the computer number 416521 stamped next to the withdrawal dated 23 September 1991. The numbers 4165 form a code used by the Commonwealth Bank to identify the branch where the transaction took place. In this instance, the code relates to the Goodna branch. The number 21 indicates the terminal that was used to process the transaction, and records at the bank confirm Tymon logged onto that terminal that day.

There can be no doubt therefore that Tymon processed the transaction. If it was not a third party transaction as claimed, then why was it processed as a third party transaction? Eight years later, Audrey Tymon still had no doubt she served a young girl that day. As she explained it, she had been in trouble shortly before this event for authorising a third party transaction that turned out to be fraudulent. She was conscious not to let it happen again.

There seems little doubt that Tymon is correct and this raises more questions than answers. It potentially confirms that Leanne was still alive around 11.15 a.m. on Monday and probably later, as she still had to return the money and passbook to Herbert Holland. Consequently, the time available for Graham to have murdered her is considerably diminished. It also raises the questions: why did Leanne withdraw money for Herbert Holland? and why he would argue that she did not?

There is one more question: why the police, according to Tymon, became markedly cool towards her when it became clear that her evidence did not support their case against Graham? When taken in conjunction with the evidence of Marjorie Rodgers, it seems likely that the young girl seen outside the Commonwealth Bank that morning was indeed Leanne.

It was not until 2006 that Crowley attempted to locate and interview Marjorie Rodgers. It was she who claimed to have seen Leanne outside the Commonwealth Bank on that fateful Monday morning. The actual police job log had specific instructions 'Locate and interview the boy RODGERS.' There was also this comment on the job log: 'The Rodgers boy went to school with HOLLAND till last year.' Apparently, mother and son were together outside the Commonwealth Bank.

At the time of going to press, Crowley has been unable to locate Marjorie Rodgers or her son. We do not even know his Christian name, which obviously makes location extremely difficult. It begs the question though: did police interview the Rodgers boy? More importantly, what was the result of that interview?

Herbert Holland and his wife had lived in their Albert Street home in Goodna for more than 30 years, but sold it in September 1992. When Graeme Crowley visited the house in 1993 and spoke with the new owner, he was told Herbert Holland specifically refused to leave a forwarding address for mail, though a forwarding address was requested.

Crowley had some difficulty tracing the Hollands, but when his doggedness paid off, Herbert maintained his story: that he had made the withdrawal personally and had been served by a male teller. He remained unmoved when it was explained to him that there were no male tellers then working at that branch. Herbert willingly produced the passbook, but said he was unable to help further as he had told police everything he knew.

Another relatively minor, but still significant error in the police case concerned the garbage bag found underneath Leanne's body. The Crown contended this garbage bag was used to contain bleeding and/or transport Leanne's body, and that it came from the Holland house.

Crowley was perplexed by the various court and police documents he had read about the bag. Crick told the court, for example, that it was not possible to test the bag for blood because it was originally tested for fingerprints and the process used destroyed any blood present, but, when Crowley examined the bag at the sheriff's office, he found it in pristine condition. It appeared to be brand new and there was not the slightest suggestion of any blood on or in the bag. When Crowley asked the police, he was told that the fingerprint section use glue vapour on the bag to highlight latent fingerprints and this could eliminate blood.

Unconvinced that such a bag could effectively carry a dead body, be tested for fingerprints and yet remain in pristine condition, Crowley followed his investigator's instinct. It was not long before he established that only two manufacturers, who had a relatively equal market share, produced the majority of all green plastic garbage bags in Australia. This particular bag was manufactured by OSO and the head office of the company was in Brisbane.

At Crowley's request the Brisbane manager accompanied the investigator to the sheriff's office at the Supreme Court where he identified the bag as having been manufactured by his company, as were other similar bags found in Leanne's house. The manager said it would be possible to find such a bag in every second household in Australia and that: 'You would be flat out carrying three house bricks in one of those bags.'

20

Identical tyre patterns

Another hurdle revolved around the two different tyre impressions found where Leanne's body was dumped – impressions said to match the two quite unique tyre patterns on Graham's car. The Crime Investigation Log recorded Crick's initial description of the tyre patterns to investigating police on Saturday 28 September thus:

> 'info from Bill Crick, scientific, that tyre impressions found at the scene are similar to the tyres fitted to Stafford's Gemini. He can only say that the treads are of the same pattern – not that those particular tyres on the Gemini have been at the scene.'

Two months later Crick claimed that the tread patterns on Graham's tyres were the same as the two tyre patterns located on the bush track and, at the trial, his evidence was that they were similar in shape and tread. Only under cross-examination did it come out that a third tyre impression that Crick could not eliminate was found at the scene. The owner of that tread pattern was never established. It appears little effort went into finding them.

What is known is that Mr Justice Derrington referred to the tyre impressions no less than seventeen times when delivering his final charge to the jury. Indeed he observed that there was a 'combination of tyre tracks that were identical with [Stafford's] car, a combination which the witness, the gentleman who changed tyres, said is a fairly uncommon combination of tyre treads.' This was compelling evidence to support the Crown case. Yet, it had not been adequately tested nor scrutinised except at the trial.

To compare the patterns found at the scene with the tread patterns on Graham's car, Crick first took photographs of the two different impressions found in the dirt. These photographs were enlarged to the point where they were of the same size as the impressions on the bush track. A small scale was placed beside the actual impressions prior to the photographs being taken to ensure that they could be enlarged to the exact size. Crick then took impressions of the two different tyre treads on Graham's car, not dissimilar to taking a person's fingerprints. These impressions were rolled onto paper and then transferred to clear plastic. These transparencies, or overlays, were then placed on the photographs and compared.

Crick told the court that the vertical and horizontal lines of the impressions matched up and that he could find no dissimilarities between the patterns on the overlays and the patterns in the photographs.

In the weeks leading up to the trial, Crick had two meetings with the then state manager for Bridgestone Australia, Rod Thomas. They discussed the number of Bridgestone tyres sold in south-east Queensland, particularly the SF340 and RD229 patterns as found on Graham's car.

Crick showed Thomas the two inked impressions that he said came from Graham's tyres. Thomas recognised the tread patterns, but told Crick it would be impossible to determine the actual tyre size merely by looking at patterns on paper. He also said there was a Brisbane company making retreads that were the same pattern as the RD229. Of interest too is that Crick had inked impressions, transparencies and a large cardboard display showing photographs of Graham's tyres over which he could lay the transparencies, yet he chose to show Thomas only the inked impressions.

When Crowley first viewed the overlays, at the sheriff's office of the Supreme Court registry in the later part of 1993, he was disturbed to find that he could not make the transparencies fit the photographs.

After reading the trial transcript and the significance attached to this evidence by the trial judge, Crowley expected to simply place the overlays over the photographs and see a perfect match between the impressions and the tyre patterns. There seemed to be some similarity with the SF340 tyre, but Crowley simply could not obtain a match with the RD229 tyre no matter how he tried. He wondered why he was apparently the first person to have this difficulty. Surely, he thought, the defence counsel had placed the transparencies over the patterns on the photographs. Surely the jurors had examined this vital piece of physical evidence during their deliberations.

When Crowley approached Rod Thomas at the Queensland head office of Bridgestone Australia and asked him to view the overlays and photographs, he was overwhelmed at the cooperation extended to him. The first Thomas knew about the existence of the overlays was in November 1993, when Crowley told him about them.

At that time, Mr Thomas had more than 30 years' experience in the tyre industry. He willingly accompanied Crowley to the sheriff's office and compared the overlays and the photographs.

Later, he gave Crowley a statement saying the tyre pattern known as SF340, taken from Graham's car, was similar to the impressions in the photographs. He could not, however, satisfy himself that the RD229 tyre pattern from Graham's car was similar to the impressions in the photographs.

Thomas felt that in the circumstances it would be proper to canvas another opinion. He told Crowley there was someone in the company's Brisbane office with more expertise than him in matters of technical comparison of tyre shape and tread patterns. Crowley was introduced to the Queensland Technical Field Service Manager for Bridgestone, David Lee, and listened as Thomas briefed him. Lee had more than 34 years' experience in the tyre industry. He warmed to the task and was keen to visit the sheriff's office to look at the overlays.

Lee presented as a cautious, energetic individual, who took a clinical approach to the matter. He asked many questions about the making of the overlays and the presentation of the evidence and told Crowley he would like to see where the impressions were made. Thomas, Lee and Crowley then went to the bushland where Leanne's body was found.

Lee also wanted to examine Graham's car; have it make impressions in the dirt and see the results for himself.

The trio collected Graham's Gemini and drove it up the dirt track off the Redbank Plains road. Lee took numerous photographs, but established that Graham's car had travelled approximately 450 kilometres since it had had new front tyres fitted, prior to 26 September 1991.

At Bridgestone's expense, new RD229 tyres were fitted to the front of Graham's car and it was driven another 450 kilometres. David Lee was intent on replicating the original condition of the car's tyres as closely as possible.

Once again they returned to Redbank Plains with the Gemini and took more photographs. These were enlarged to actual size, again at Bridgestone's expense, and comparisons were made with transparencies obtained from the inked impressions taken from the tyres.

Many hours were spent on this project by Bridgestone staff as more trips to the sheriff's office ensued. Finally, Lee concluded that the tyre impressions found at the crime scene did not match the tyre patterns on Graham's car.

Crowley was certain this was a major breakthrough in his investigation. He did not believe that the evidence of Thomas and Lee could be ignored. They were employed by the manufacturers of the tyres in question and between them had more than 60 years experience in their field.

David Lee swore an affidavit in 1995 for Graham's lawyer, Mr Carew. He concluded that the RD229 (front) tyre pattern on Graham's car was not identical with the impression in the dirt at the crime scene. While he noted some similarities, he also noted dissimilarities:

I strenuously disagree with the evidence given by Charles William Crick, Police Scientific Officer, at the trial of Stafford that: (1) he 'could not find any differences' between the shape and tread patterns shown on the enlarged photograph and in the inked impression; (2) he was in a position to have told the investigating officer 'the treads are of the same pattern'; and (3) in comparing the inked impression and the transparent overlay photocopy of the inked impression that 'you can see that the lines in both directions line up and are the same width and distance apart'.

Commenting on the SF340 tread pattern Lee deduced they were not identical. He went on to say that even if it could be established that it was an SF340 tread pattern in the dirt, it could be one of eight different sized tyres made in that pattern. He noted too that there are other tyre manufacturers who made tyres sufficiently similar in shape and tread pattern to the RD229 and the SF340 to be indistinguishable. He disagreed with Crick that with respect to the SF340 overlay:

You can see that the zigzag lines line up across the width of the tyre and also the vertical lines.

Further, he strenuously disagreed with the evidence of the tyre fitter, Tony Bashforth, that there was no other tyre company that made tyre patterns the same as the Bridgestone RD229 and SF340.

Rod Thomas provided a sworn affidavit stating that the tyre impressions at the scene were not identical with the RD229 tyres on Graham's car. He went so far as to say it was highly unlikely, if not impossible, that the impression in the dirt was caused by Graham's front tyre.

In relation to the other impressions made at the scene, Thomas formed the view that the impression was similar to the SF340 pattern on Graham's car, but that it was impossible to state that the tread pattern at the scene was made by a Bridgestone SF340 tyre.

The appeal court dispensed with this evidence very simply. The judges concluded that Lee lacked the opportunity of making a direct comparison between the tyre tread and the impressions made at the crime scene; whereas Crick had the advantage of being able to compare the transparencies with the original impressions in the soil.

Severe cracks were appearing in crucial areas of the prosecution case. Crowley had produced a substantial and clear dispute of the tyre evidence, the sightings of Graham's car at the scene were doubtful enough to be discounted and the Crown's own forensic experts were now challenging the prosecution case. Crowley was demonstrating that evidence, which should have been properly tested before Graham was charged and brought to trial, was failing to stand up to a thorough examination – an examination that should have been carried out as part of the original investigation, not years later.

21

Alive on Tuesday

As Crowley reinterviewed witnesses about sightings of Leanne when the prosecution said she was dead, even more cracks in the case appeared.

A long-time resident of Goodna, Christine Lawrence, claimed that she had seen Leanne in a car parked next to her at the Goodna shopping centre at about 9 a.m. on Tuesday. She said that Leanne was with a young male, aged about twenty. Christine described the car as an old Escort or 'a bomb'.

At the time of Leanne's disappearance, Lawrence was a bar attendant at the Kerwick Hotel at Redbank. She claimed she knew Leanne's father Terry, because he drank at the hotel occasionally and regularly played darts there. Lawrence said Leanne used to accompany him on some of the darts nights.

After seeing a newspaper article concerning Leanne's disappearance on the Thursday of that week, she spoke to a male friend and told him about the sighting two days earlier. The man volunteered to ring the police on her behalf and later told her he had done so. Lawrence was never contacted by police in relation to her information.

There is no official record in police files of the contact by her male friend and the police deny the call was ever received.

Another Goodna resident had contacted police to say that she had received a telephone call at about midday on Tuesday 24 September, from a girl she believed to be Leanne. The caller was looking for the woman's daughter, who was a friend of Leanne's and had gone to the party with her the previous Friday night.

This woman was also never asked to give a statement and was never contacted again by police. The defence obtained a statement from her years afterwards, but her evidence was dismissed by the Court of Appeal. The woman could not satisfy the court that the telephone caller was Leanne. This incident and the sighting by Lawrence, however, do raise the issue of whether there were other witnesses who contacted police, but were never interviewed.

Another significant part of the prosecution case was that Graham was lying about his arm injury, and did not injure himself working on his car.

To support their case, a police motor mechanic, Sergeant Carlton, gave evidence that he inspected the underneath of Graham's car on Wednesday 2 October, shortly after Graham's arrest. Carlton noted a new shock absorber had been fitted on the left-hand front side. He could not find any marks or scratches to the under body components or the floor of the vehicle consistent with it slipping off a jack.

Clearly, part of the police case was that a reasonable person could assume that some sort of telltale mark would be left if a vehicle slipped off a jack in the manner claimed. It was curious, given that the police were trying to show that Graham had lied, that they did not consider it necessary to take photographs nor video footage of his car to prove there were no scratches. Had photographs been taken of the allegedly pristine under body of the car as observed by Carlton, the matter would not now be an issue.

Jean Stafford claims that after Graham's car was released to them in November 1991 they parked it in their garage where it stayed until the trial. The first time she or her husband were aware of the evidence of the police inspection of her son's car was when it emerged at the trial.

After court recessed the day that Carlton gave his evidence, Eric and Jean went home and inspected the left-hand underside of

Graham's car. To their disbelief, they found scratches they thought could be consistent with the car slipping off the jack and immediately told their next-door neighbour, pointing the scratches out to her. This neighbour later confirmed that Eric and Jean would not have had time between arriving home and calling her to make the scratch marks themselves.

Showing more forensic knowledge than the police, Eric and Jean telephoned a friend who came straightaway and videotaped the scratches. The following morning they told defence counsel Clark of their find, but he decided not to raise the matter in court.

In December 1992 Crowley arranged for a mechanic to inspect the underside of Graham's car. The mechanic made a statement saying he found two marks that were in his opinion consistent with the car slipping off a jack. This evidence was similarly dispensed with by the Court of Appeal.

22

Missing murder weapon

The alleged murder weapon was another baffling piece of prosecution evidence. It is not clear exactly how many hammers Graham owned and the actual number may never be known. Both Graham and Melissa Holland insist that he only ever owned one hammer. However, it appears certain that the jury were left with the damning impression that Graham's hammer went missing the same day as Leanne.

The significance of this is obvious. The Crown alleged Graham used a hammer or similar instrument to beat Leanne to death. The pathologist told the court she believed the injuries inflicted on Leanne were consistent with being caused by a hammer. Graham's hammer was a Cyclone brand, black-headed tool and for several weeks prior to the murder he had been using it to hang pictures to brighten up the room he and Melissa shared, so it had been stored on the bedside table.

Whether the police found it in the bedroom or in the boot of Graham's car is uncertain, but they did find a hammer and took possession of it. This is confirmed by a reference to a hammer in the record of the interview conducted immediately before Graham's arrest.

Detective Fynes-Clinton told Graham: '… in the boot of your car we have found a hammer. It's a wooden-handled hammer with a metal head, it's painted black, and it's a Cyclone brand.' Graham agreed the description was correct and, when asked if the hammer was his, said it was. That was when Fynes-Clinton dropped his bombshell, revealing forensic tests had found blood traces on the hammer. Graham's voice was choking with emotion when he replied: 'No way – no.' The hammer was never produced at the trial. Indeed, prosecutor Bullock at one point asked of Graham: 'The police haven't got it. Can you offer an explanation as to where it might be?' Graham replied: 'No, I haven't got it.'

Another aspect of the case not yet satisfactorily resolved involves the Vietnamese neighbours at number 72 Alice Street. The ageing occupants spoke little English. The police log indicated they had been interviewed and said they were at a funeral all day on the Monday Leanne went missing and were therefore unable to help with any information. Crowley enlisted the services of a young Australian woman whose parents came from Vietnam and who could speak both English and Vietnamese. The woman was studying law at the time and today is a solicitor of the Queensland Supreme Court. She went with Crowley to the house where she acted as an interpreter and spoke to the couple, both in their seventies, in their own language. Their grasp of English was obviously limited and Crowley wondered how the police had interviewed them, as there was no mention in the running sheet of using interpreters.

The couple told Crowley's interpreter that they were at home on the Monday that Leanne went missing. The husband said he was in the garden at about 9 a.m. when Leanne came to the fence carrying a puppy. He had a conversation with her and told her he was planting a paw paw tree. She in turn told him that she was on school holidays. Leanne then left, heading in the direction of the convenience shop and he never saw her again.

The man also told the interpreter that at about 10.30 to 11 a.m. that day he saw the young man who lived next door working on his car in the backyard, near the clothesline. The man was lying under the side of the car on a piece of board. He pointed to a large piece of board that was near the back stairs of the house next door and said it was similar. The young man worked on the car for about 15 minutes, and then he drove away. The Vietnamese couple were home all day and did not hear any noise from Leanne's house. The man also said that the police visited them and they told them exactly what they had told the interpreter. The couple were adamant that they did not go to a funeral on that Monday and, as an aside, they described the young man next door as a polite and gentle man who never caused any trouble.

All these alleged sightings and the refutation of the vast bulk of the forensic evidence appeared to have no effect on the appeals processes. One of the justices who voted against Graham's appeal summed up the saga in these words:

> Apart from the unreliable evidence of sightings of Leanne on or after the afternoon of 23 September 1991, there remains no evidence casting doubt on the opportunity that Stafford had to kill Leanne on that afternoon. There is no credible explanation for Leanne's blood being on Stafford's bag in the locked boot of his car, to which only he and Melissa had access, other than that he killed Leanne. And the evidence of other blood not capable of being identified, the maggot and the hair also found in the boot, of the missing hammer, of the lies told to the police and of the car sightings near where Leanne's body was found add weight to this.
>
> Although the new evidence may make it unlikely that Stafford killed Leanne in the house and left her body in the boot of his car for two days I am satisfied that there is no significant possibility that a jury acting reasonably, even with that evidence before it, would have doubted that he killed her.

23

Blood in the house

Some people associated with this case believe that the bloodied items in the boot of Graham's car may have been deliberately or accidentally placed there. It is possible that Leanne walking down the front stairs, to show her father her cut foot in August, might explain the blood on the corner of the blanket owned by Melissa. It might also explain how the blood came to be on the rag and on the tool bag. Perhaps one of the family had a nose bleed.

There was after all never any evidence presented to the court to show that these three items were always in the boot of Graham's car. Two of the items did not even belong to him. The principle of exchange may attribute for all of them. It is more difficult, however, to decipher an innocent explanation for the maggot – similar to the ones found on Leanne's body – being in the boot of his car. This was significant and damning evidence against Stafford.

Crowley spent many hours investigating the disturbing possibility that someone may have planted evidence in this case, including the police.

Being an ex-cop he discounted such a possibility as unlikely and repugnant to his own experiences as a police officer. Having reported his findings to Eric and Jean, however, they still find it difficult to accept that this incriminating evidence was found in their son's car or that their son was responsible for it being there.

The significance of this evidence was not lost on the many appeals courts that have dealt with the case. These courts have focused, not only on the maggot, but also on the blood on the items in the boot. Without question, it was always a key reason the appeals by the defence team were consistently denied. Various judges made comment on the blood and went so far as to conclude that Graham could have been convicted of killing Leanne solely on the blood traces in his car boot. This was very compelling evidence in favour of the Crown and clearly a major reason why Graham was found guilty.

A specialist employed by the Queensland Health Department, Mr Leo Freney, carried out a complete and thorough review of all the scientific evidence in the Stafford case in 1995, following an approach by Richard Carew. Freney had access to and examined all the original case material submitted to the forensic science laboratory that was still available. Freney had more than 33 years' experience as a forensic scientist and was the supervisor of the original blood analyst, Kristine Bentley. He had given expert evidence in criminal trials almost 1000 times and was unquestionably one of Australia's leading forensic scientists. A newspaper article about him in the year 2000 described him as 'Queensland's own Quincy' – a reference to a US television series based on forensic science. In 1996, he prepared an affidavit containing the results of his review. Copies were given to both the defence and prosecution solicitors.

After reviewing the evidence, he formed the opinion that Leanne was not murdered at her home. From the police videotapes of Crick's examinations, Freney concluded that the jury would have taken the view that a large quantity of blood was scattered throughout the house when, in fact, only a small quantity was found. He concluded the jury would have been misled about the amount of blood found in Graham's car and on items in it. He further surmised that Leanne's blood did not get onto the tool bag in the manner suggested by the Crown.

Freney swore that the evidence concerning hair found in the boot was unsatisfactory and pointed out again that Leanne's hair had not been dyed. His final statement was that:

the overall state of the forensic science evidence available in this case, when fully explored and compared with the contentions put forward by the prosecution, is extremely unsatisfactory and highly likely to have led to the jury drawing incorrect inferences and conclusions.

Freney was called by the defence to give evidence at the appeal in 1997, despite being under considerable pressure not to by prosecutors. Freney said he was interested only in the scientific evidence, not whether the accused was guilty or innocent. He is a remarkable man, prepared to stand up and speak out for what he believes in. Despite his reputation, experience and forceful opinions, the Court of Appeal dispensed with his evidence thus:

Mr Freney's evidence, if accepted, makes it unlikely that Leanne was killed in the house and her body placed in, and left for some days, in the boot of the appellant's car.

Of course, that says little about whether the appellant [Stafford] killed Leanne; it goes only to whether he killed her in the house and placed – and left – her body in the boot of his car.

No doubt, there are other scenarios, consistent with the appellant's guilt, which would explain the presence of Leanne's blood on the bag in the boot of his car. He may have enticed her to go with him to a remote location, perhaps at or near where her body was found, and killed her there. Her blood on the bag and, perhaps, other items in the boot, may be explicable as coming, after her death, from his person or from the instrument that he used to kill her. He may later have returned to the scene to move her body to a more remote location. This may also explain the presence of the maggot and the hair in the boot.

This speculation flies in the face of all the evidence gathered and presented at the trial, as well as numerous appeals. The viewpoint of the justices can be seen by the following statement: 'Moreover it is difficult to think of a credible explanation for the presence of

Leanne's blood in the boot of Stafford's car which is consistent with his innocence.'

Despite one of Australia's leading forensic scientists strenuously challenging the prosecution case, his opinion was conveniently ignored. More significantly, this was an expert witness usually called by the prosecution, not the defence.

However, this is not the end of the question marks hanging over the forensic evidence. At the murder trial, Crick was asked whether he detected any odour when he searched the boot of Graham's car on that Wednesday in September.

Bearing in mind the Crown alleged that Graham had secreted Leanne's body in the boot of his car for up to two days, the question was valid. Crick responded by saying that he detected no odour from the boot during any search of the car. Dr Ashby supported Crick's claim by telling the court she would not expect an odour from the dead body of a child aged twelve. This statement seems contrary to all the literature on decomposition. Indeed, Richard Carew approached the Director of the Forensic Science Centre, Dr Anthony Ansford, a qualified medical practitioner employed by the Queensland Health Department for 22 years on this question.

Dr Ansford was asked his opinion of the evidence and stated that there was no difference in the odours of a decomposing body on the basis of age.

He expressed the opinion that, had the body been stored in the boot as described and given the circumstances described to him, there would have been an odour in the boot of the car. He went further and said it was his opinion that Leanne's body would have leaked a significant quantity of blood during that time. Wrapping the body in something such as a garbage bag would have been insufficient, he said, to mask the flow of blood or the smell. He also examined the tool bag on which blood had been found and said the bloodstains were inconsistent with the prosecution case.

Regrettably, the Court of Appeal dispensed with Dr Ansford's evidence.

24

Justice denied

Crowley's final report and statements were passed to solicitor Richard Carew. Using the report to prepare sworn affidavits, the solicitor presented a Petition for Mercy to the Governor of Queensland on 18 September 1996, seeking a review of the case. The matter was referred to the DPP who in turn referred the matter to the Queensland Court of Criminal Appeal in February 1997. Further time passed awaiting the court's decision. By a majority of two to one, the Court of Appeal dismissed Graham's petition on 23 September 1997. The irony of this date was not lost on Eric and Jean. Despite that six-year time lapse, the public gallery of the court was packed. Around 50 family members and friends of both Graham and Leanne tried to cram into a space designed for twenty people. The President of the Court took the unusual step of allowing members of the public to sit on chairs within the court proper, rather than have them standing at the rear. A court officer commented that he had not seen such interest in an appeal in his 30 years' experience in the justice system.

The court, in its decision, summed up the Crown case in the following words:

The Crown case against the appellant was a strong circumstantial one, the main features of which were:

a) On September 23, 1991, the day on which, on the case, the deceased girl was murdered, the deceased and the appellant had been left alone in the home in which they both lived with the deceased's father and sister, the latter of whom was living in a de facto relationship with the appellant.

b) Blood was found on a number of items in the boot of the appellant's car, the blood was shown to be of the same type as the deceased's, a type which was found on one-and-one-half per cent of the Australian population.

c) Also found in the boot was a strand of hair similar in length, colour and texture to that of the deceased girl and a maggot of the type and age found on the deceased's body. Furthermore, swabs taken from inside the boot lid and lip had human blood on them, which could not be grouped.

d) Blood consistent with the deceased girl's was found in a number of places in the house.

e) Car tracks of the same type as those of the appellant's car were found on the track, which led to the body; however, tyres with tracks of this kind were not uncommon.

f) A hammer, which was kept beside the appellant's bedside table, was missing; such an instrument was consistent with having caused the injuries to the deceased's head.

g) The appellant told lies to the interviewing police.

h) A fold-up chair usually kept in the boot of the appellant's car was found in the spare room in the house, the appellant claiming that he had put it there after cleaning the car on September 23.'

The prosecution also adduced that Graham sustained an arm injury they alleged was caused by murdering Leanne. Furthermore, his car had no damage to the chassis, inconsistent with his claims of his movements on that day. In the court's opinion, no new evidence had been presented to counter the Crown case.

Defence lawyers claimed there was now strong evidence to suggest he did not and could not have murdered the victim. Such evidence was not available, they said, at his original trial. On the basis of that evidence, he should be given a retrial. The court found that Graham had received a fair trial, the trial judge had not erred in law; and the so-called new evidence was probably available at the time of the original trial. In all these circumstances, he was not entitled to a new trial.

The fact, however, that the case was again before the appeal court and had been refused enabled Graham's lawyers to again take the matter to the High Court and, in the process, create Australian legal history. Never before had anyone twice applied to the High Court to quash the same conviction. Graham's family had no confidence that justice would at last be done on 17 April 1998 when the matter finally came before the court. They had lost all faith in the legal system, but doggedly pressed on. Only one of 23 listed applications for special leave to appeal was granted. One of the justices had this to say:

> But the things that were not possibilities were: the mallet was missing, there was no explanation that your client could offer for the blood or the maggot in his own car, he had injuries to his arm which were unexplained, there were car tracks that were consistent with his car, he put out the garbage, which was not his practice, and that is just a few of them. I think it is a very, very strong Crown case, especially the maggot.

It took just 23 minutes for the High Court of Australia to decide Graham's fate. His conviction and life sentence were confirmed. He had exhausted every avenue of legal challenge and taken his fight as far as he could. Only a miracle or eventual parole would see Graham released from gaol.

The High Court verdict also signalled the end of media interest in the Stafford case. Journalists, particularly around south-east Queensland, had maintained a vigil, regularly reporting any development in the case. However, once the highest court in the land had handed down its decision, Graham became yesterday's news and it would have taken a brave journalist to approach an editor suggesting a special interest story. Initially, the case had attracted more media interest than usual because of Leanne's age and the prosecution's claim of sadomasochism being involved. DNA evidence too was in its infancy and much of the Crown case relied on forensic evidence. The usual print and television coverage of the investigation, arrest and trial followed. Throughout 1993, 1994 and 1995 various newspapers throughout south-east Queensland ran stories on the case. Sunshine Coast newspapers took an interest because the family lived locally. Western suburbs papers were naturally interested, too.

Investigative journalist Darrell Giles, of Brisbane's *Sunday Mail* ran a series of articles. During the same period a commercial channel broadcast nationally a television documentary on the case. Alexander McLeod-Lindsay, who suffered a 30-year nightmare after being gaoled for the attempted murder of his wife, told reporters at the time that he was closely following the Stafford case and he offered this advice to Graham: 'Don't give up ... keep on fighting.'

25

A profiler's opinion

Although not yet widely acceptable in Australian courtrooms, a criminal profile on Leanne's likely killer was possible. Criminologist Paul Wilson explored this possibility through his profiling contacts in Australia and America. Some aspects of criminal profiling have been admitted in evidence, but the field is still not well-developed. There are no universally accepted standards nor a recognised professional body to accredit the experts who practise it. Still, Wilson was keen to explore the possibilities that a profiler might yield and was able to secure the services of Brent Turvey – one of America's best-known criminal profilers and crime-scene reconstructionists.

Turvey has worked on a number of high profile murder cases in the United States (such as the Beltway Sniper and the West Memphis III cases) and is the author of *Criminal Profiling: An Introduction to Behavioral Evidence Analysis* which is the best selling textbook on profiling world-wide. So, while Brent Turvey was here in Australia teaching courses to police and other investigators on the techniques of crime scene reconstruction, victimology and other aspects of criminal profiling, he was able to peruse all the case materials on Leanne Holland's death and, once he returned to America, he carefully considered this material and later sent a comprehensive report on the case.

Turvey pointed out in his report that the forensic evidence – with blood samples found in the boot of the car and in the bathroom of the victim's home, as well as the maggot found in Graham's vehicle – suffers from a crucial weakness. Specifically, the bloodstains and the maggot were not checked using modern DNA testing techniques to reliably match them to the samples collected from Leanne's body. He was also particularly critical of the way that scientists for the prosecution presented their evidence at the trial in regard to the maggot evidence as well as a lot of other forensic evidence.

He then provided a timeline outlining the events that happened which succinctly reveals that there were at least eight sightings of Leanne from the time that Melissa and her father had left for work by 7.45 a.m. on Monday until she was reported missing to police at 5.45 p.m. on Tuesday. Delving into the police investigation, Turvey notes that:

> … many of the investigative tips and leads in the Queensland Police Major Incident Job Log were not investigated subsequent to [Graham's] arrest. Notations beneath many of these tips and leads read simply 'This information is no longer relevant to the Holland murder as Graham Stuart Stafford has been arrested for the murder of Leanne Holland'. Tips and leads that were not further investigated include a 40-year-old neighborhood male, previously convicted of sex offences, who was allegedly approaching neighborhood girls.

They also include a report of a man with blood on his hands and jeans who entered a shop on 25 September 1991 asking for money. This becomes significant upon consideration of the weak circumstantial evidence that provided the foundation for Mr Stafford's arrest.

Turvey also undertook a victimology analysis, which is 'a thorough study of all available victim information', and estimated that Leanne had both a high lifestyle risk and a high incident risk for being a victim of violence, for the following reasons:

- history of socialising with age-inappropriate males;
- history of sexual promiscuity;
- history of hitch-hiking and related activities;
- history of getting into vehicles with strangers;
- lived in an area with known sex offender;
- history of spending time away from home unsupervised.

His report was highly critical of some of the autopsy findings. For example, the alleged burn marks on Leanne's body were never fully investigated to establish whether they were burns or abrasions as was suggested in one part of the forensic pathology report. Similarly, he calls into question the vague statements surrounding the description of the peri-anal wound which he says is possible to have resulted from decomposition of the body, not necessarily from a dull knife as was put forward by Dr Ashby. The third area he takes issue with is the characterisation of Leanne's killer as a lust murderer:

As the victim was dead when the injuries in question were inflicted, and sexual gratification on the part of the offender may only be assumed (there is a lack of injury to sexual regions of the body, no evidence of sexual penetration, and equivocal evidence relating to anal injury as described above), there is no foundation for either classification.

In summary, it is apparent to this examiner that the opinions relating to crime reconstruction and crime classification offered by the pathologist are equivocal, reductive, incomplete and under-informed. They are subsequently not based on hypothesis testing, consideration/investigation of alternate theories, or other reasonable means of forensic inquiry.

He concludes by offering some investigative suggestions, including:
- In the victim's home the baseboard of the bathroom vanity should be removed and the area examined for any bloodstains.
- An unknown hair was found in the trunk of Graham Stafford's car. This item should be examined and compared to known samples of victim hair by a hair and fiber expert. Additionally, suitability for STR DNA analysis on any root material should be

determined. In addition to this, mitochondrial DNA testing is possible using the hair shaft if all else fails.

- A single short, non-pubic hair can be visualized on the victim's buttocks, just to the right of the ruler in place to measure other injuries. It should be determined if this hair was recognised and collected. If so, this item should be examined and compared to known samples of victim hair by a hair and fiber expert. Additionally, suitability for STR DNA analysis on any root material should be determined.

- There is no mention in the case materials provided to this examiner of fingernail clippings being tested in this case, though they were collected and sent to Kristine Bentley. They should be examined for tissue. If tissue is present, STR DNA analysis should be performed.

- A clump of hair was found in the bathroom bin in the victim's home. ... This item should be examined and compared to known samples of victim hair by a hair and fiber expert. It should be determined whether or not this hair was dyed, and if so, what color. Additionally, suitability for STR DNA analysis on any root material should be determined. In addition to this, mitochondrial DNA testing is possible using the hair shaft if all else fails.

- A plastic bag was found underneath the victim's body. This can and should be tested for latent fingerprints using the technique known as Vacuum Metal Deposition. It should also be compared to any unused bags in the victim's home. Not only for brand, size and type, but for individuating characteristics such as the rifling of the plastic as it passes through the machine. Bags that have been torn apart may be reliably connected in sequence from the same roll using this manner of examination.

- According to statements made by Terrence Holland and Graham Stafford, Leanne left home at 9.30 a.m. to meet a friend at the shopping center. While some effort was made to interview female friends of the victim to determine whom she was meeting, very little effort was made to interview or locate age-inappropriate male friends who the victim was known to socialise with.

A list of her known male friends should be made and interviewed as suspects in this case.

26

The fight goes on

After the final appeal was heard in 1998 Crowley was more than ready to let the matter go. He had been involved in the case for almost seven years, the majority of it at his own time and expense. It was not that he felt Graham Stafford was guilty; just that he had done as much as one man could do. In fact after the final appeal nothing much happened for about three years. The issue was dead in the water. Everyone had lives to get on with, incomes to earn, other issues to deal with. The media had also moved on, so there was not the continual inquiry regarding what was happening with the case. Stafford had exhausted his legal processes. The story was going nowhere.

Paul Wilson kept the story alive through his position as Professor of Criminology at Bond University on Queensland's Gold Coast. He incorporated the case in his lectures when teaching students in his popular Miscarriages of Justice classes within the Law and criminology faculties as well as to Forensic Science students.

He invited Crowley to travel to Bond University and lecture to the students at least once each semester. Classes were then tasked with reviewing the evidence and identifying areas that could be developed further. Students were invited to undertake their own research and submit papers on the subject.

Wilson's miscarriage class was taught with Professor Eric Colvin, an expert on the criminal appeal process. There were always a number of currently-serving police officers in the class, many of whom were initially sceptical about the case being a wrongful conviction. However, year after year the scepticism on the part of these police officers transposed into a belief that a miscarriage of justice might well have occurred. This feedback, together with fellow criminologist Robyn Lincoln's view that the case deserved a wider audience, was the impetus for eventually writing a book.

Crowley agreed that a book was necessary and was confident of what he had discovered over the years. He had essentially eliminated all the Crown evidence and was sure that this could all be adequately explained in a book.

There was one problem, however, that kept niggling away with him – the blood evidence – but even here he felt that there was an explanation. There would have been transference of blood anyway, because the accused and the deceased were living together. Leanne had also cut her foot prior to her death and had bled all the way down the front stairs. To top it off, two of the three items found in the boot of Stafford's car did not belong to him anyway.

There was the evidence from Dr Ansford, the Head of the Queensland Forensic Science Institute, who determined that the blood from the red and black sports bag was deposited when fresh and not from a decomposing body because such blood would have a significantly different appearance and a foul smell. Remarkably, fate intervened and proved even more to both Crowley and Wilson that the blood evidence was not as damming as the courts had suggested. In March 2006, Crowley was lecturing to a group of students at Bond University – at Wilson's invitation. He was introduced to Angela van Daal who co-taught a course with Wilson on forensic science.

Van Daal was the forensic scientist who had originally tested the blood in 1991 at the request of the Queensland prosecution. It transpired that in 1991 she was sent samples of blood by Queensland Police and was only ever asked to say whether the samples were the same as Leanne's blood, which they were. Dr van Daal was not told that Leanne's father, sister and brother were also living in the house. She was always under the impression the accused and the deceased were the only persons living in the same house. This changed everything, she excitedly told both or them.

The blood could also have come from another member of the Holland family, but she was never asked to test for this. Crowley was able to confirm that blood samples were taken from the other Holland family members, but never forwarded for analysis. Crowley remembered and commented on the fact that the brother, Craig Holland (now also deceased) had also bled profusely inside the house after a drunken brawl in a nearby hotel in which he had received a deep and nasty gash to his arm, which he wrapped in a tea towel.

Van Daal said that from her experience, there was a 25 per cent chance that the blood shown to be the deceased's blood, was in fact not her blood at all. Yes, the blood was 'family blood', but it may well have come from another family member. Van Daal further stated that she was never asked to comment on the amount of blood recovered from the crime scene – just a few drops – as she states this would be inconsistent with the evidence already gathered.

Meanwhile, the media interest in the continuing story gathered momentum. Perhaps it was the fact the story would not go away; or perhaps the journalists knew their readers loved a murder mystery. *The Sunday Mail* reported on developments in the case and published regular, high-profile articles, which is surprising considering the case was then fifteen years old. On 23 April 2006, Darrell Giles wrote:

Convicted killer Graham Stafford is set for a dramatic early release. The 42-year-old, sentenced to life in 1992, could be granted parole within months. Stafford, who has always strenuously denied killing the sister of his then-fiancée, was not expected to be released for several years. He had been in a *Catch-22* situation because he continued to proclaim his innocence, prison psychiatrists said it meant he had shown no remorse and should be denied parole. But sources told *The Sunday Mail* he had been a model prisoner and there was widespread support from prison authorities for his bid to clear his name.

The publicity propelled Crowley to seek a meeting with the Attorney-General and in April 2006, Crowley had a two hour meeting with the then Queensland State Attorney-General Linda Lavarch. Ms Lavarch confirmed she had been following the developments in the case and was monitoring it closely.

At the conclusion of the meeting, she indicated Graham Stafford should apply for a pardon and such application would be given full and proper consideration by her department.

The publicity continued. On 21 May 2006 the readers of *The Sunday Mail* were provided further startling revelations regarding the case:

A key prosecution witness in the Leanne Holland murder is set to turn the controversial case on its head. Legal experts say astonishing new information could free convicted killer Graham Stafford after almost 15 years behind bars. Forensic scientist Angela Van Daal gave crucial evidence that helped convict Stafford of the horrific 1991 sex slaying of the Goodna schoolgirl at his trial the following year. But she now says blood identified as Leanne's – a central piece of the police case – could have come from another family member.

Following further media stories, Graham Stafford was given early release from prison. The story made front page news in *The Sunday Mail* on 4 June 2006 with the headline:

STAFFORD PARDON BID AFTER EARLY PAROLE
The parents of convicted killer Graham Stafford have told of their joy at his release from prison and say he is more determined than ever to clear his name. The 42-year-old, sentenced to life in 1992 for the brutal sex slaying of schoolgirl Leanne Holland, 12, was given full parole this week – four

months earlier than authorities had indicated. Stafford is now living with his parents Jean and Eric on the Sunshine Coast. 'Obviously we are very pleased, very happy, very relieved,' Mrs Stafford said yesterday. 'I think we are all a little bit stunned. … as if we cannot believe it has happened.' Stafford's early release came after Police Minister Judy Spence told *The Sunday Mail* in April; that he would not be eligible for parole until serving a minimum 15 years in jail, which would have been late September.

Corrective Services found Stafford full-time employment on the north side of Brisbane. He was given a labouring position in a large company. While the management knew of his background, fellow employees were blissfully unaware of his past. Corrective Services had placed severe restrictions on Stafford including a total ban on contact with the media. Meanwhile Radio 4BC, a local Brisbane radio station, took up the case. With Greg Carey, a well-known and respected commentator taking particular interest.

During his daily afternoon program, he invited listeners to call in with their comments and was deluged with talkback on the subject. So much so that both Crowley and Wilson were regularly interviewed on air, along with the Queensland Attorney-General and some notable forensic experts who expressed their concern regarding the quality of the evidence presented by the Crown.

However, even the experienced Carey was surprised when the jury foreman from the original trial called in to express his concern about the conviction. The foreman was later to appear on the *7.30 Report*, a national current affairs television program produced by the ABC, which prompted the Queensland Government to express its concern over jurors debating the validity of jury convictions.

It transpired that several truck drivers employed by the same company as Stafford were regular listeners to Greg Carey's afternoon radio program. It was not long before they connected the Graham Stafford on the radio to the Graham Stafford working in their factory. While Stafford was unable to discuss the matter because of the ban imposed upon him, the story became well known in local circles and Stafford became somewhat of a celebrity. It is worthy of note that Stafford continues to be employed in the factory at the time of publication and is well liked by management and fellow staff.

Perhaps even more bizarre was that both Graeme Crowley and Graham Stafford used the nearby train station to commute for work and their schedules would sometimes cross. Their meetings were friendly and relaxed though they did not know each other that well, having only met on a few occasions. Stafford was always insistent that they not talk about the case; he was concerned that any breach of his parole conditions on discussing the case would mean a revocation of his parole and a return to prison, a situation he indicated he did not want. However, he was always happy to talk football or other sporting topics.

Jean and Eric Stafford were under no such restrictions, but they too were reluctant, almost fearful of discussing the case. They regularly expressed concern that any criticism they might make may result in Graham being returned to prison. While it was pointed out to them their beliefs were irrational, they would not be moved. They turned down a number of requests from media outlets for their story, some quite lucrative. Because of their English origins, an English-based media outlet was willing to pay considerable money for their account of the case. Once again the offer was politely declined.

While his parents would not publicly comment on the case, they did privately state they had seen some changes in Graham after his release from prison. He was more introverted than before his arrest. He was not as relaxed as he used to be, more restless, and lacking self confidence.

It appeared to Jean and Eric as though their son had become conditioned to being told what to do and when to do it. He was reluctant to make a decision on his own. On top of this, it was increasingly apparent that Graham was worried about the possible deportation to England hanging over his head. He had absolutely no idea what he would do if he were forced to live in England by himself.

He was, however, getting on with his life and has since bought a car to get around in. His mother states that his main interests are again his car and music. He maintains the same friends, and some new ones, since his imprisonment.

So, despite Crowley's efforts to move on from the story, it gathered momentum and developed a life of its own. Media outlets continued to monitor the saga and write articles. Loose ends, too, kept appearing and it was necessary to tie them up, which wasn't easy and, as Crowley quipped to a journalist on one occasion, 'it is difficult to conduct a one-man murder investigation'.

With continued media attention, more people came forward with information. Some were quite interesting and exciting, others not so dramatic. Information included various snippets which implicated one or more persons in the crime. Not unexpectedly, no one came forward with information implicating Graham Stafford. While much of the information was tantalising and tempting to follow up, Crowley had to continually remind himself his role was not to solve the crime (although that was tempting), but to locate evidence which corroborated the fact that Stafford had not committed it.

However, some of the information coming forward was exceptional and simply could not be ignored. A classic example here was the story of the male person who supposedly confided in his then-girlfriend that he had murdered a young girl near some beehives in western Brisbane in 1991. The girlfriend then told her housemate what the boyfriend had said. Apparently, the male was so violent that neither woman took the matter any further at that time because of the fear of retribution from him. About 12 months after this confession, the male was involved in an armed robbery that resulted in his imprisonment for a lengthy period. During the robbery, both he and his accomplice were shot and wounded. The story would have ended there, but the housemate had never forgotten.

She contacted Crowley in January 2006 after seeing a media report on the case and believed this was the murder the man had confessed to. She related her story, but added she could now not even remember the name of the male nor the name of her then-housemate. She stated she had neither seen nor heard from either party since that time and she had no idea of the current whereabouts of either person. Nor did she want to, she hurriedly added. She informed Crowley that they were all using and dealing in such quantities of drugs during that period she could not have gone to the police even if she wanted to. The central theme of identification she was able to supply was the robbery. She told Crowley that police had burst in on the offender while his girlfriend was removing shotgun pellets from his head.

Crowley was able to make inquiries into the robbery using old newspaper records and, with the assistance of his friend, the reporter Darrell Giles, he was able to obtain the name of the robber. When Crowley 'googled' his name on the internet he was stunned to find several recent newspaper articles concerning him. The robber was charged with a murder in January 2005 in Hobart, Tasmania. The deceased male was killed using an axe and a hammer. On 14 October 2005 the offender pleaded guilty to murder and was sentenced to nineteen years imprisonment. The judge had this to say during sentencing:

The circumstance that makes your crime remarkable is your conduct after the initial blow that resulted in the victim's death. Immediately that blow was struck, the appalling nature of your conduct and its likely consequence should have been apparent. You not only failed to respond with compassion, you did not even desist. You continued to strike the victim with the back of the axe and obtained a hammer with which you also struck him. Your initial blow severely fractured the victim's skull. Additional injuries caused by your subsequent blows included a compound facture of his left humeris, a fracture of the mid-shaft of his left femur, a fracture of the distal portion of his left femur, extremely marked bruising on his right wrist, and a substantial number of other bruises, abrasions and lacerations. You are 39 years of age. Since the age of 16, you have been an alcoholic and addicted to amphetamines. You have also experimented with heroin to the point of overdosing on that drug. Your record includes convictions for crimes involving violence in respect of which you have, on three occasions, served sentences of imprisonment, the last of which sentences was imposed in 2001.

The arresting officer later confirmed the offender had convictions for violence in Tasmania, Western Australia and Queensland. He went on to say the offender was extremely violent toward females.

Crowley was unsure what to do with this information. He knew Queensland Police were unsympathetic and disinterested; the information was of no use to any subsequent appeal unless he was able to obtain a confession from the suspect. Other articles found through the Internet search listed the name of the killer's Tasmanian Legal Aid solicitor. Crowley wrote to her, asking if she would visit the killer in prison and raise the matter of the Holland killing. He appealed to her position as an officer of court and a duty to see justice done.

Crowley figured that if the killer showed sufficient remorse to enter a guilty plea to a charge of murder, he may just be willing to discuss any involvement or knowledge of the Goodna murder. He received no reply.

Crowley then wrote to the prisoner direct, in Risdon Prison in Tasmania. He asked him if he had any knowledge of the murder of Leanne Holland. He appealed to his sense of justice by pointing out it was unfair that a person with no criminal convictions (as opposed to his own lengthy history) should have to serve prison time for an offence he did not commit. He even included a stamped addressed envelope in the forlorn hope he would receive a reply. Crowley could not help, but smile at the irony of another first – interviewing a murder suspect by letter. Not surprisingly, he received no reply.

Although it is pure speculation to say this person was involved in the Holland murder there are a remarkable number of coincidences. Crowley wondered whether there was any connection between this male and the police informant with the violent criminal past who figures so prominently in this case.

27

A grave miscarriage of justice

In mid-2006, Paul Wilson – acting on behalf of the Stafford family – started approaching solicitors he knew with a view to preparing another appeal to the Governor of Queensland.

The Governor has the power within the Queensland Constitution to pardon the petitioner. In most instances though, the Governor passes the matter to the Attorney-General, who in turn refers the request to the Court of Appeal to deal with the matter. (some people irreverently refer to this process as 'passing the buck).

Wilson knew there was now only one further opportunity and there would be no second chances. He was fussy about who would be asked to prepare the appeal. He was also aware that considerable publicity would be generated if the appeal was successful and that, lacking money to finance such an appeal, the possibility of a case which would generate a high public profile might be of interest to a progressive lawyer.

A number of lawyers showed interest in representing Stafford, but the one who stood out was Joe Crowley (no relation to Graeme Crowley) who was a part-time Professor at Bond University where Wilson himself worked. The two had never met before, but over a series of meetings initiated by Wilson it was clear that Joe Crowley was the right person for the job. Though relatively junior as a barrister he showed considerable enthusiasm for the case and a detailed knowledge of what the appeal process would involve.

'It is going to be hard,' he told Wilson, 'even if the Governor refers the case back to the appeal court, the court is a very hard nut to crack – they seem always to want fresh evidence and, although fresh evidence was provided in both the second appeal and the first petition to the Governor, Stafford still remains inside prison.'

As it turned out Joe Crowley's motivation for taking the case had nothing to do with any publicity that might result from the brief. Rather, the lawyer felt that a grave injustice had been done in the Stafford case and that the criminal justice system had made a grievous mistake. It was therefore up to the system to rectify this monumental error and, as a lawyer working in the system, he had a moral obligation to try and do something about it.

Joe Crowley, together with criminologist Robyn Lincoln and some of Bond University's best criminology and law students, spent hundreds of hours putting the complex petition together. Whether all this work comes to anything or just comes up against the same legal brick wall that the other appeals and petition met remains to be seen. 'All you can do is your best,' Wilson told Crowley. 'After all, most of us know that the courts always deliver a verdict, but not always justice'.

Wilson was able to announce in August 2006 that work had started on the appeal. But it progressed slowly. There was much ground to cover and Joe Crowley had to get it right. When he saw the volume of work that had been assembled and the huge amount of evidence that had been uncovered, he was confident that a fresh appeal would be successful. It was some months before he was able to come to grips with the huge array of documents in his possession. By then too, he had an in-depth knowledge of the evidence that had been available and presented to the Court of Appeal in 1996/1997.

At that point he confided to both Paul Wilson and Graeme Crowley that he was no longer supremely confident of success. He was stunned by the huge volume of new evidence that had been placed before the court in the previous petition and yet that appeal had been denied.

That may well be the problem with this case. Appeals have been won and lost on one piece of evidence, one flawed argument of case law, one seemingly insignificant comment made by the trial judge during summing up to the jury. The problems with this case are many and considerable.

There is not just one piece of evidence that is in question, but many; virtually the whole Crown case is challenged in one way or another; indeed it would be easy to sum it up as 'how could so many people get it so wrong for so long'. Perhaps therein lies the problem – educated people, who should know better, actually do not accept that so many could get it wrong for so long and in doing so ignore the evidence that has been placed before them. It is now anticipated that the new appeal result will not be known until approximately September 2007. By then this case will have dragged on for sixteen years, almost to the day.

There are only three possible outcomes. Firstly, the appeal will be denied (one would like to think this unlikely given the significant evidence to support it) and the original conviction upheld. In that case, Stafford's conviction will stand. He will most likely be deported and the Queensland Police Service (QPS) will have a strong argument not to reopen the investigation.

The second possible outcome is that the conviction is quashed (least likely) and Stafford is granted a pardon. This would be the most favourable outcome for Graham and his family who have stood by him for so long. However, the QPS would probably argue against reopening the case on the grounds it is too old and the majority of evidence destroyed. In that case Stafford would always be known as 'the killer who beat the conviction on appeal'.

The third and we believe most likely outcome is that the matter would pass from the Governor to the Attorney-General's Office who would refer the case back to the Court of Appeal (as happened in 1997). The court would then have to determine whether they refuse or uphold the appeal.

In the event the appeal is upheld, the court would have to decide whether to quash the conviction or order a retrial. It would be most unlikely the matter would go back for a new trial. The Director of Public Prosecutions (DPP) would argue that the case is too old, too much evidence has been lost or destroyed, witnesses have died and so on. It would also be unlikely the QPS would be inclined to reopen the investigation. Again Stafford would be remembered as the killer who beat the conviction on appeal. If the appeal was denied then it would have the same effect as the Governor refusing the appeal – Stafford would be deported.

In February 2007, Graham Stafford lodged a complaint with the Crime and Misconduct Commission, the independent watchdog in Queensland. The CMC deals with all complaints against government employees, including police. Graham Stafford alleged various criminal offences occurred during the investigation into the murder for which he was convicted. CMC investigations have been known to take months and even years to conclude.

Whatever the outcome of the appeal and the complaint to the CMC, it is apparent there has been a grave miscarriage of justice, not just on behalf of Graham Stuart Stafford, but also on behalf of Leanne Sarah Holland. Neither person has been well served by Queensland's justice system. Neither person can rest until this murder is properly and thoroughly reinvestigated, which is unlikely ever to happen.

One of the most disappointing lessons from this case is that we as a society appear not to have learned the lessons from the past. Almost twenty years ago, Paul Wilson conducted one of the first analyses of Australian miscarriages of justice (published in the *Australian Journal of Social Issues* in 1989). Three years later he co-authored, with *Sydney Morning Herald* journalist Malcolm Brown, *Justice and Nightmares* (UNSW Press, 1992) – a book that looked at both the successes and the failures of forensic science.

In both publications it was pointed out that the reasons for miscarriages of justice in major cases were often the same. These reasons included hasty and badly organised police investigations in order to obtain a quick arrest and the over-reliance on forensic science evidence, especially when a motive cannot be established.

The archetype of this genre is clearly the case of Lindy Chamberlain. In the Chamberlain case no adequate motive was established nor were the forensic techniques employed accurate or appropriate enough for the scientists to come to their conclusions.

As Wilson and Brown note in *Justice and Nightmares*, in the Chamberlain trial of 1982 scientific evidence was so dominant that it quite overshadowed the final plaintive appeal of the Chamberlains' counsel, Mr John Phillips QC, later to be elevated to Chief Justice of the State of Victoria. Mr Phillips told the jury that 'mothers don't normally kill their babies'. Justified as Phillips was to make this argument, he lost the day to the forensic scientists.

That was in 1982, since then we have been assured by the forensic experts that their systems and techniques have improved and that they have 'got it right'. But the reality, as the Stafford case reveals, is that they have not got it right and that any conviction that is solely based on forensic evidence has to be looked at with great suspicion.

The investigation into the murder of Leanne Holland has been shown to be sadly lacking in most areas. Indeed, the police were so sure that they had arrested the right man for Leanne's murder that they ignored other witnesses, irrationally eliminated alternative suspects, and carried out superficial and sometimes clumsy examinations of the available evidence.

We would like to think that similar police investigations are unusual in this country. Unfortunately, our combined experience suggests that one-sided and sloppy investigations are quite common and that the numbers of miscarriages of justice that result from these procedures are considerable.

Such miscarriages are almost impossible to overturn, if only because the combined resources of the police and the prosecution overwhelm the scant resources available to the defence. Information has been provided to the authors by Queensland police officers that the Stafford investigation has been used — withing policing circles – as a benchmark, a showcase of what can be done in investigations where there are no confessions, no witnesses and no motive. We can only hope that the media storm generated by our independent investigations will cause the QPS to reconsider its training procedures.

We have worked on this case for years without financial compensation because the conviction of Graham Stafford highlights the continuing sores that plague our justice system. Who knows how many other innocent men and women languish in gaol because they lack the resources or the contacts so necessary to prove their innocence? The conviction of Graham Stafford for the brutal murder of Leanne Holland is based on evidence that is even more flimsy and misleading than the evidence that convicted Lindy Chamberlain. We contend that it was physically impossible for Graham Stafford to have killed the young girl and that the forensic evidence that convicted him was clearly inaccurate and misleading. Until Graham's conviction is reversed it will remain one of the most startling examples of how a man can be wrongly convicted of murder simply because the justice system believes in both the invincibility of forensic science and the impartiality of police investigations in major crimes. Inevitably therefore, Graham's conviction throws into doubt the many other cases in Australia's legal history where convictions have been obtained based solely on forensic evidence, without corroborating witnesses or the credible establishment of motive and opportunity.

Graham Stafford served fifteen years in prison – from the age of 27 to 42. He has lost the best part of his life. We do not believe that Graham could possibly have murdered Leanne, but let's put that point aside for a moment.

We believe that our investigation into his case clearly demonstrates that he did not receive a fair trial and his case was not fully and properly considered by the appeals courts. Indeed, Graham found himself in a *Catch-22* situation where, because he continued to proclaim his innocence it meant that in the eyes of the corrections system he was showing no remorse.

Prior to his release a report by a psychiatrist employed by corrective services said in part: 'Mr Stafford should not be recommended for any leave of absence or resettlement into the community and can only be re-considered in the future after he has changed his stance of denial.' It seems that the negative media interest generated by our investigation forced Corrective Services to rethink their position in relation to Stafford.

On a personal level the emotional cost to the Stafford family has been enormous. Jean Stafford, though proud of the way that her son has stood up to his ordeal, is worried about the effect that it has had on him. Although she told us that her son hasn't changed much from the outside, she herself, as a mother usually does, has noticed some inner changes. 'He doesn't want to go out now,' she said, 'and he doesn't talk about what happened in gaol'. She worries that Graham, being small, suffered grievously in gaol, but he won't talk about it.

Jean and Eric, Graham's father, have also suffered. 'This experience has ruined our life,' she said 'it took years to realise that you just have to go on living and you keep believing the truth will come out.'

Though bitter towards the police and the justice system generally, Jean and Eric believe that the saga has taught them all to be more compassionate and not to believe everything you read in the papers. She also is a lot more sceptical about people in authority, whether they are in politics or the justice system.

Despite her anger towards many of those in power there is one positive feeling that she takes away from the drama that has obsessed her for so many years. So many ordinary people appear to believe in Stafford's innocence, including, she tells us, many of the staff who knew Graham in prison and who so readily provided references of good character for him for job applications or parole board hearings.

In the end, however, her cynicism towards the justice system remains strong. 'The authorities must believe that it is not possible that an innocent man could be put in prison,' she told us, and though optimistic that the new petition to the Governor might bring results she is trying not to put too much hope on it. Referring to the last petition she said, 'blind Freddie could see that he didn't do it, but it still got nowhere.'

Of course a mother's endorsement of her son's innocence is hardly evidence that he did not kill Leanne Holland. But, in our view, the weight of evidence that we have uncovered and presented in this book clearly shows that he did not – indeed could not have – killed the young teenager.

That is precisely why we contend that, until Graham Stafford is exonerated, this case will remain an indelible blot on this nation's system of criminal justice.

28

The aftermath

The road to legal justice is certainly a long one. It took three years from the time it was decided to launch yet another appeal for the hearing to take place. Joe Crowley, the young barrister persuaded solicitor David Swanson and the highly experienced Mr Douglas Savage SC into acting for Stafford at the appeal hearing. All three had worked tirelessly on the case pro bono and had constructed a carefully-worded petition to the governor of the state seeking a referral back to the court of appeal. This was the third appeal. Two others had failed to make a difference, so Joe Crowley knew that the petition had to be exemplary. In addition to gathering all the material together and presenting it in a logical and fresh manner, there were also political hurdles to deal with, due to both the governor and the attorney-general changing during that period.

The petition itself was hardly a short document. Indeed, it was 30,000 words long and on 30 November 2007, Joe Crowley drove himself and the petition in his early model Saab through the large gates of 'Fernberg', the Governor's official residence. Any hopes he had of tea and scones with the Governor were dashed when he was met by a burly security guard who took the petition and seven folders of accompanying documentation from him and sent him on his way.

Eventually, it was announced that the petition had been successful and that there would be a date set for the appeal court judges to go over the evidence. This did not occur until Thursday, 5 November 2009. It was held in the Banco Court

– the largest venue of the Supreme Court precinct near the river in Brisbane because officials knew that many would want to attend. They were right. Lawyers, students, media, the Stafford family and supporters filed into the courtroom cheek-to-jowl with some of the police who had investigated and charged Stafford.

The argument that Stafford's lawyers ran with was that Stafford deserved an acquittal from his previous conviction. Proving his actual innocence was almost impossible given that the police had refused to carry out further investigations and that appeal courts rarely gave judgements of innocence, only ones that argue that a previous verdict of guilt was 'unsafe'.

The atmosphere was tense as Douglas Savage argued in his calm but penetrating style that all the forensic evidence that convicted Stafford did not actually show that he had committed the murder.

He painstakingly went through the maggot evidence, the tyre marks at the scene where the body was found, and the blood found on the items in Graham's car and tore these apart piece by piece. However, the prosecutor, Mr Michael Copley SC, for the Department of Public Prosecutions, argued that even if the jury had heard some of the problems with the forensic evidence they still would have convicted Stafford. 'There was no miscarriage of justice' he claimed.

Afterwards, a small party was held at the Grosvenor Hotel in George Street – a familiar drinking hole for the legal profession. We gathered in the downstairs area – which paradoxically resembled an underground holding cell for prisoners awaiting their trial to commence.

Despite the décor, the mood was elevated but nevertheless tinged with anxiety, for even though a huge milestone had been achieved – the first time that a murder conviction had returned to the court of appeal for a third occasion – no-one was really convinced that we would win the case. Graham gave a sober but thoughtful speech where he thanked those who had supported him over so many years and especially his family and Graeme Crowley. He knew however, like everyone else in the room did, that there was still more anxious waiting ahead.

On 24 December 2009, seven weeks after the hearing, Graham Stafford sat in the court to hear the result of the appeal for his conviction for the murder of Leanne Holland. In a two-to-one majority verdict, all three judges agreed that the appeal should be allowed and his conviction quashed. Two of the judges found that there was sufficient evidence for a new trial to take place, but one of the judges, Justice Catherine Holmes, came out far more strongly and said that she would have acquitted Stafford.

What this verdict meant was that Graham Stafford was no longer convicted of the murder of Leanne, but remained accused of that crime. The next step in the long legal road was for the Director of Public Prosecutions to consider whether to, yet again, charge Graham Stafford with the murder of his girlfriend's younger sister all those years ago and to proceed to a retrial or not. Given the difficulties that any person faces in attempting to get a conviction overturned by a Queensland appeal court this was a major victory, but not a complete one.

The stigma of still being accused of one of the most horrendous crimes in Australia's history still hangs over Stafford and that stigma will only be removed by a total exoneration.

As he heard the appeal court give their verdict, Stafford, who had spent so many years fighting for his innocence, dropped his head and tears began to flow. He had held himself together for so long but this was a moment of release. He always knew that he was innocent of this terrible crime and now at last there was some legal recognition that this indeed was the case.

For those of us who have joined with the Stafford family over the decades, it was a poignant moment to hear on car radios and to see on the evening television news the lead stories proclaiming this victory. What a timely Christmas gift this turned out to be for Graham, his family and the extended legal and criminological family that supported them through this journey.

Interviewed by Darrell Giles from Brisbane's Sunday Mail,

Jean Stafford said that she had noticed that Leanne's father, Terry Holland, was in court when the appeal was being heard. Giles, who has consistently reported on this story over many years, quoted Mrs Stafford as saying 'I felt for him ... I've got a daughter too'. Expressing her sorrow for what had happened to young Leanne, she sympathised with the Holland family having to go through countless court cases about Leanne's murder. But, she said 'I am sure if it was their son who they believed to be totally innocent, they would do the same as we have done.'

Perhaps the most poignant reaction to the verdict in the Stafford case was given by Graham himself. In February 2010 he travelled to the Gold Coast to talk to the Miscarriages of Justice class at Bond University taught by Paul Wilson and criminal law expert, Eric Colvin.

This was the first time that Graham had talked publicly about his case and his reactions to the charges, the court cases he had endured, and his time in prison. He was not bitter or angry but rather philosophical about what had happened in his life. He described some of the drudgery of prison life, the accusations early on by some fellow inmates about him being a 'rock spider' – the lowest of the low – and the bashings that he suffered. On the other hand, as his time in prison went on, he noticed that more and more prisoners as well as prison officers began to think that he might be innocent, with some even encouraging him to keep fighting.

Though relatively calm while describing his life inside, his calmness gave way to tears as he discussed the effect of his conviction on his family and especially on Jean and Eric. 'They were marvellous', he said. 'I was just lucky to have parents who knew that I couldn't kill anyone and backed me for so many years.'

Graham then answered a barrage of questions from students who were fascinated to see how a man who had suffered one of Australia's greatest miscarriages of justice had handled such a psychologically devastating experience. He addressed the questions with honesty and frankness, seemingly oblivious to the cameras of the ABC's Australian Story crew who were present in the lecture theatre filming the third part of the trilogy they had produced on the Stafford case.

Everyone in that lecture theatre, indeed everyone connected with the case, realised that the Stafford story was far from over. There were many questions still to be answered: would the DPP re-charge Stafford with the murder of Leanne Holland? If not, how would Stafford go about obtaining compensation for the nearly 15 years that he endured within Queensland's prison system?

Most lawyers connected with the case believe that the DPP would not put Stafford on trial again. After all, most of the evidence had now been demolished, the forensic samples appeared to be lost in the bowels of the justice system, and there was compelling argument as Justice Holmes noted, that Stafford did not have time to kill Leanne Holland. As the Judge succinctly stated, it would have been almost impossible in the 80 minutes that Stafford could not account for on that fateful Monday to find Leanne, kill her, dispose of the body, clean himself up, and then turn up at his friend's place 'looking plausible'.

Indeed, most legal observers argued that the DPP would simply claim that there was little point in re-trying Graham because he had already served a murder sentence so there was no public interest that could be gained. Cynically, the same observers noted that such an action by the DPP would make it extraordinarily difficult for Graham Stafford to obtain compensation for the years of pain and suffering he had endured during this long and sorry saga.

When the history of compensation pay-outs for other Queensland victims of miscarriages of justice is examined, they are probably right. Most, like Kelvin Condren – who was wrongfully convicted of a murder he could not possibly have committed because he was already in police custody at the time of the crime – took years to receive what was generally considered a paltry amount of money. Others, like Terry Irving, who was found guilty of an armed robbery – a verdict that eventually was castigated by the High Court and for which the role of the Queensland justice authorities was severely condemned by the United Nations Human Rights Commission – have still not received any compensation after a decade.

The cynics were correct. On Friday the 26 March 2010, Mr Moynihan, the Director of the DPP, announced that after consulting with the police and the family of Leanne Holland, a retrial would not go ahead for several reasons. These included that Mr Stafford had served his sentence, had been deemed fit for release back into the community and that 20 years had passed since the murder, which had affected the state of the evidence. The same cynics argued that the evidence had been fatally affected when the police investigation had begun all those years ago.

After the publication of an earlier edition of this book and again at the time of the recent successful appeal, the Stafford story attracted considerable media attention with the Sunday Mail, 4BC as well as ABC TV and Channel 10 all updating their audiences with how the case was progressing. Major newspapers such as The Australian, Brisbane's Courier Mail and the Queensland Times also gave extensive coverage to the case, sometimes raising hard questions about the reliability of the original police investigation. As a result, both Crowley and Wilson received countless calls or emails with supposedly new evidence about who the real killer was. However, little information of significant value was ever provided. Crowley once observed to Wilson that what was interesting was that from all these calls and emails, no-one came forward with evidence to support the DPP and Police position that Graham Stafford was the killer.

The major question remaining, of course, is who did kill Leanne Holland? Graham Stafford did not do it and that must mean that the murderer is still out there – a person or persons who committed one of Australia's most vicious murders. We have canvassed two people in this book who we think deserve further police investigation. One is a young man who, six weeks after the death of Leanne Holland, sexually molested and drowned Julie-Ann Lowe in a creek barely a kilometre from Leanne's home. We have pointed out that this young man knew Leanne and that he had an extremely disturbed and violent background.

Then there is the sadistic predator who knew the Holland family and allegedly had even taken Leanne for rides in his car. Strangely, he told Darrell Giles of the Sunday Mail that he helped police solve the killing by working undercover with them. This man, as we have pointed out, served a seven year sentence for rape and incest before being released in 2003. The victims of his crimes, his two daughters, told Graeme Crowley that they had been raped in the same spot where Leanne's body was found and that he had shown them photos of Leanne's corpse and threatened them with a similar fate if they spoke out. Who will investigate these possibilities or any others that may arise?

The police have said categorically that they have no intention of re-opening any investigation unless 'new, credible and admissible evidence comes to light'. Surely the evidence we have uncovered in this book gives some credible directions for a new investigation? Alternately, if the police do not hold a cold case inquiry then such new and admissible evidence is likely to remain buried forever. Similarly, the Crime and Misconduct Commission have found nothing wrong with the original police investigation. This is despite the fact that dark shadows hover over at least one of the detectives involved in the original Stafford case. How then is this crime to be solved?

Of course, there is the real possibility that this crime will never be solved and that the stigma of being a murderer will hang over Graham Stafford's head for the rest of his life. This is a stigma that remains with many miscarriage of justice victims regardless of whether they are exonerated by the courts or not – a stain that lingers in their own mind and those of others every day of every week of every year. Given Graham Stafford's resilience and courage, we are quietly confident that he will cope better than most.

Short bibliography

Naughton, M. (2005) 'Redefining miscarriages of justice: a revived human-rights approach to unearth subjugated discourses of wrongful criminal conviction', *British Journal of Criminology*, vol. 45, pp 165–182.

Poveda, T. (2001) 'Estimating wrongful convictions', *Justice Quarterly*, vol 18, no 3, pp 689–708.

J. Langdon and P. Wilson (2005) *Current Issues in Criminal Justice* Vol. 17, 2, 2005, pp 179–202.

Brown, M. and P. Wilson (1992) *Justice and Nightmares*, UNSW Press, Sydney.

Blackburn, E. (2001) *Broken Lives*, Hardie Grant Books, Victoria.

Wilson, P.D., Treble and R. Lincoln (1996) *Jean Lee: The Last Woman Hanged in Australia*, Random House, Sydney.

Noble, R. and D. Schiff (2000) *Understanding Miscarriages of Justice*, Oxford University Press, Oxford.

Carrington, K. et al (eds) (1991) *Travesty! Miscarriages of Justice*, Academics for Justice, Macquarie University, Sydney.

About the authors

Professor Paul Wilson OAM

Currently Chair of Criminology at Bond University, Professor Paul Wilson has been an academic administrator, criminologist and media commentator and columnist. He was Foundation Dean of Arts at the Queensland Institute of Technology and Dean of Humanities and Social Sciences for eight years at Bond University, Australia's first private University.

Prior to these appointments he held academic appointments at the University of Queensland and visiting Professorships at American Research Institutes and Universities. Professor Wilson is a Fulbright Scholar and held the prestigious Library Fellowship at Rutgers University's School of Criminal Justice.

Professor Wilson is the author of 25 books on crime and related social issues, and of hundreds of academic journal articles or research reports on criminological issues. For six years he was Director of Research and, at times, Acting Director at the Australian Institute of Criminology. Some of his books include Black Death White Hands, Murder in Tandem and Justice in the Deep North (with Carole McCartney and Robyn Lincoln).

One of his abiding interests relates to miscarriages of justice. His book (with *Sydney Morning Herald* journalist Malcolm Brown) *Justice and Nightmares* reflects this as does *Who Killed Leanne Holland?* In the academic journal, *Current Issues in Criminal Justice*, he recently summarised most of the major cases of miscarriages of justice in Australia.

As a columnist he wrote weekly columns for *The Herald-Sun* for six years and fortnightly columns for *The Courier-Mail* for a further six years, as well as contributing to newspapers such as *The Australian*, *The Sydney Morning Herald*, *The Age* and *The Sunday Age*. He frequently comments on crime and criminal justice issues on radio and television.

In 2003 Professor Wilson was awarded the Order of Australia Medal for 'services to education, particularly as a writer and lecturer in the field of criminology and to the community through raising public awareness of social justice issues'.

Graeme Crowley

Graeme was a member of the Queensland Police Force for twelve years, reaching the rank of Detective Senior Constable. He gained a 'Favourable Record' for a complex criminal investigation he conducted. He served in areas as diverse as the notorious Fortitude Valley, Motor Squad and Townsville CIB. He regularly travelled to Palm Island to investigate murders, rape and other serious crime.

After leaving the police, he operated his own private investigation business for ten years. He rarely accepted private work, preferring to work for Insurance Companies and law firms. It is therefore unusual, and perhaps a twist of fate, that he agreed to meet the Stafford family.

Graeme is currently a national manager for a leading debt collection company.

Always a believer in a 'fair go', Crowley felt that Graham Stafford had received anything but a fair go in his treatment at the hands of the justice system. He also believes that Leanne Holland has not had justice done. His primary motivation in writing this book is to see the murder investigation of Leanne Holland reopened and the real offender/s brought to justice for their crime.

This is Graeme Crowley's first book. He is currently investigating other unsolved murders in Australia.

www.ingramcontent.com/pod-product-compliance
Lightning Source LLC
Chambersburg PA
CBHW040137270326
41927CB00020B/3422